BRADY'S CIVIL WAR

BRADY'S CIVIL WAR

A collection of memorable Civil War images
photographed by Mathew Brady and his assistants

WEBB GARRISON

Introduction by ALAN AXELROD, PH.D.

THE LYONS PRESS

A SALAMANDER BOOK

PUBLISHED IN THE UNITED STATES BY THE LYONS PRESS
123 WEST 18 STREET
NEW YORK, NY 10011
www.lyonspress.com

© SALAMANDER BOOKS LTD. 2000, 2002, 2008
AN IMPRINT OF ANOVA BOOKS COMPANY LIMITED
10 SOUTHCOMBE STREET, LONDON W14 0RA

ISBN 978-1-59921-315-6

2 3 4 5 6 7 8 9 10

CREDITS

PROJECT MANAGER: RAY BONDS
DESIGNER: INTERPREP LTD
PICTURE RESEARCHER: ANNE LANG
ARCHIVAL PHOTOGRAPHER: ROLF LANG
COLOR SEPARATION: STUDIO TEC
PRINTED IN THAILAND

ADDITIONAL CAPTIONS

ENDPAPERS: BRADY LEANS AGAINST A TREE WHILE APPARENTLY USING A
REMOTE CONTROL TO OPERATE THE CAMERA'S SHUTTER TO MAKE A
PHOTOGRAPH OF A GROUP OF UNION OFFICERS.
PAGE 1: GENERAL U. S. GRANT IN CASUAL POSE, WEARING A MIX OF
LIEUTENANT GENERAL AND MAJOR GENERAL UNIFORMS.
PAGES 2-3: A COMPANY OF UNION INFANTRYMEN POSE PROUDLY FOR THE
CAMERA IN FRONT OF CAMP.
PAGES 4-5: BRADY STANDING BESIDE ARTILLERY BEING READIED FOR
ACTION, JUST MOMENTS BEFORE REBEL SHELLS SCREAM OVERHEAD.

PUBLISHERS' NOTE

THE PUBLISHERS ARE GRATEFUL FOR THE ASSISTANCE OF THE U.S.
NATIONAL ARCHIVES AND LIBRARY OF CONGRESS, AND THE PRIVATE
COLLECTIONS WHICH HAVE CONTRIBUTED PHOTOGRAPHS FOR THIS BOOK.
THE PUBLISHERS HAVE CHOSEN TO PRESENT THE PHOTOGRAPHS AS SUPPLIED,
AND NOT TO ALTER THEM (OTHER THAN SIZE) BY AIRBRUSHING OR ANY
OTHER ARTIFICIAL MEANS, PREFERRING TO LEAVE ON THEM MARKS CAUSED
BY CRACKS AND SCRATCHES ON THE ORIGINAL GLASS NEGATIVES, OR
BLEMISHES AND IDENTIFICATION NOTES MADE BY ARCHIVISTS OVER THE
PERIOD OF ALMOST ONE HUNDRED AND FORTY YEARS SINCE THE
PHOTOGRAPHS WERE TAKEN BY MATHEW BRADY AND HIS ASSISTANTS.

THE AUTHOR

WEBB GARRISON SPENT MUCH OF HIS EARLY CAREER
IN ACADEMIA, AS A DEAN AT AN IVY LEAGUE
UNIVERSITY (EMORY IN ATLANTA, GEORGIA) AND
PRESIDENT OF A VERY OLD COLLEGE IN ILLINOIS
(MCKENDREE). DURING THESE YEARS HE ALSO
WORKED AS A FREELANCE WRITER FOR MAGAZINES IN
THE UNITED STATES, WHICH PUBLISHED MORE THAN
A THOUSAND OF HIS ARTICLES AND FEATURES. HE
HAS PUBLISHED APPROXIMATELY SIXTY-FIVE BOOKS, OF
WHICH MORE THAN A DOZEN CONCERN THE
AMERICAN CIVIL WAR, AND HE HAS BEEN A GUEST ON
SEVERAL HUNDRED U.S. RADIO TALK SHOWS AND
NATIONAL TV PROGRAMS.

CONTENTS

INTRODUCTION

Mathew Brady has "done something to bring home to us the terrible reality and earnestness of war. If he has not brought bodies and laid them in our door-yards and along the streets, he has done something very like it . . . a terrible fascination . . . draws one near these pictures . . ."
—"Brady's Photographs," *New York Times*, October 20, 1862

The Swiss historian Jean-Jacques Babel famously estimated that in the roughly fifty-five hundred years that make up the recorded history of the world are to be found an aggregate of no more than 292 years of peace. Nevertheless, only a small fraction of the human beings who lived through more than five millennia crammed with violence ever experienced war personally, close-up, and at firsthand. Until very recently, war, although virtually continuous in the world, was for most people a remote occurrence. Many heard about it. Some read about it. Very few actually saw it.

This paradoxical situation began to change in 1855, when the British photographer Roger Fenton took approximately 350 photographs of the troops, officers, and battlefields of the Crimean War. Although early photographers made some portraits of the officers and men who fought in the United States–Mexican War of 1846–1848—including images of the young officers who would, years later, become the senior commanders, North and South, of the Civil War—it was Fenton's work that gave many people their first glimpse of actual war. He did not portray the action of battle, but, for the first time ever, the faces of the men who fought were photographed where they had fought, as was the landscape of battle in the still aftermath of combat. The outbreak of the Civil War in America

prompted Mathew Brady and his staff of photographers to follow in Fenton's footsteps and do for Americans even more—far more—than Fenton had done for the people of Britain.

Most historians of technology agree that photography was invented in the late 1830s by the Frenchman Louis Daguerre in collaboration with Joseph Nicéphore Niépce, Daguerre having created the first "daguerreotype" in 1837 and the two men jointly patenting a complete photographic system in 1839. The daguerreotype process yielded beautiful images, but it was cumbersome, expensive, and, because it was a direct positive process, it produced nothing from which duplicate "prints" could be made. Daguerreotypes were essentially one of a kind. The only way to make a copy was to point the camera lens at a finished daguerreotype and make another.

To get around some of the limitations of the daguerreotype, Fenton, in 1855, used the calotype process, which had been introduced more than ten years earlier by the British photographer William Henry Fox Talbot. In this process, paper coated with silver iodide is put in a camera and exposed. The exposure to light decomposes the silver iodide, breaking it down into silver and leaving iodine as a free element. The photographer chemically develops the exposed paper using solutions that wash away the excess silver iodide and oxidize the pure silver, which turns black, resulting in a negative image of whatever was photographed. Another solution is used to "fix" the image, rendering it more or less permanent. The negative is then pressed against another piece of treated calotype paper, exposed to sunlight, and the paper is developed (using the same process that produced the negative), yielding a positive. The advantage of the calotype is that the negative can be used to create any number of positive copies. The disadvantage is that calotype images are less sharp and less beautiful than daguerreotypes because the positive must be printed through paper, and even very thin paper defuses and degrades the image to a significant degree.

For the photographer in the field, making calotypes was a far more practical proposition than making daguerreotypes. The materials were lighter, cheaper, and not nearly as fragile; nevertheless, making calotypes outside of a studio still involved formidable problems. As with daguerreotypes, the relatively insensitive photographic emulsion required long exposures of five minutes or more in bright sunlight. Although

LEFT: *Washingtonians had to have bridges over the Potomac River in order to get into Virginia. The capital's noted Long Bridge—soon to be crossed by troops headed toward invasion of Rebel territory—took Brady and his entourage out of the capital when he headed toward what became Bull Run battlefield.*

portraits were possible—though subjects had to remain uncomfortably frozen for many minutes—action scenes were out of the question. Moreover, exposed calotypes had to be developed immediately, which required a portable darkroom. Fenton's photographic expedition to the Crimea was thus something of an epic of agony. He brought with him a trained assistant—one Marcus Sparling—and a servant as well as a large, lumbering van that held his equipment and served as his darkroom. The heat of the Crimean battlefield made preservation of the processing chemicals as well as the developed images a particular challenge, and Fenton himself was plagued by injury (he broke several ribs in a fall) and illness (he endured a bout of the cholera that was endemic to the conflict).

By the time Mathew Brady and the other photographers in his employ took to the field to cover the American Civil War, significant technical strides had been made. In 1851, the British photographer Frederick Scott Archer discovered that collodion, a solution of nitrocellulose in ether or acetone, could be used to coat glass plates for making photographs. The emulsion was far more sensitive than that used on daguerreotypes or calotypes, which meant that exposures were reduced from minutes to a matter of seconds—although exposure times were still much too long for most action shots. When used on glass plates, the process produced a negative, which could easily be duplicated—and because the substrate material was glass rather than paper, there was no degradation in the quality of the image, which was crisp and sharp. Despite these major advantages, collodion photography, which was also called "wet-plate photography," remained highly cumbersome, especially in the field. To begin with, the glass plates were even more fragile than daguerreotype plates, let alone calotype paper. The glass had to be carefully packed,

both before exposure and after processing, to prevent breakage, especially when being transported in a jolting wagon over a corduroy or washboard road. Before a photograph could be made, the photographer had to carefully clean the glass plate, since even a minute quantity of dust, hair, or other debris would spoil the image. Next, he flowed a light-sensitive silver iodide or silver bromide solution, mixed with collodion, over the plate until it was thoroughly and evenly coated. The treated plate was then immersed in a bath of silver nitrate for three to five minutes before it was taken to the camera and exposed. Once exposed, the plate had to be removed and developed immediately, while still wet. After development in an iron-based solution, the plate was fixed—the image made permanent—

by immersion in a bath of potassium cyanide or sodium thiosulfate. The fixed plate was quickly varnished with a solution of gum sandarac, alcohol, and lavender oil to protect the very delicate emulsion.

The entire process—from sensitizing the plate to exposing it to developing, fixing, and varnishing it—had to be completed within the space of a few minutes. In the field, this meant traveling with a portable darkroom close at hand, almost certainly with a staff of able assistants. Without them, the photographer would have to run back to his darkroom after each and every exposure; with assistants, he could hand off his exposed plates as they were made. That still left one vexing problem. The chemicals used at every step of the process were hazardous—either deadly poisons, highly flammable (even explosive), or both.

It is little wonder, then, that "Brady's Civil War" appears to us as mostly static, an array of portraits, both in the studio and on the field, individual portraits and group portraits—some impressively large—and scenes following battle, including fields of the dead and buildings, even whole city blocks, reduced to ruins.

There are very rare exceptions that hint at action in real time. A photograph Brady or one of his operatives took during the Battle of Fredericksburg in the course of a burial ceasefire shows a group of Confederates on the far side of a ruined bridge across the Rappahannock River (p. 250); it is the only Civil War photograph of Confederate personnel taken from the Union side while a battle was as yet undecided.

Artillery batteries were favorite subjects not only because the impressive guns were especially photogenic, but because of the relative lack of movement among gun crews awaiting the order to fire. These photographs nevertheless often convey the very verge of action, if not the full action itself, as in the photograph on pages 76–77 of a Union battery during the siege of Petersburg, Virginia, or that of another Petersburg battery, belonging to the 1st Pennsylvania Light Artillery, on page 85.

Even more formal portraits sometimes unexpectedly reveal the essence of life. Brigadier General Joseph "Fighting Joe" Hooker stood in frozen full-length profile beside his elegant mount, "Whitey," who kept his head as nobly still as that of his master, but the horse could not restrain his tail, which therefore appears as a ghostly blur (p. 17).

Even with the collodion emulsions that made photography in the field a practical possibility, action, vigorous action, what we think of as life at its most unguarded, immediate, and real, was invariably reduced to a ghostly blur.

This was a fact of photographic technology as it existed in the 1860s, and it was a fact that profoundly influenced the aesthetic sensibility of Mathew Brady, his employees, and his colleagues, limiting what photography could depict, yet also giving to the Brady images a distinctive aura of heroism and poignancy. Most of the photographs in the field that include people occupy an aesthetic twilight between a carefully composed and posed work of art and a nearly instantaneous documentary record. The effect is by turns stunning, impressive, and haunting, as we observe a succession of real-life actors in momentous and violent history, who barely pause to assume, at the photographer's behest, positions that would not be out of place on a sculptured frieze from ancient architecture.

In large part a product of the state of photography at the time, this effect was nevertheless no mere accident of technology. Brady and the other photographers he worked with were prepared to make genuine documentary art out of the limited means available to them. The result was images at once of the moment and yet timeless as well.

Mathew Brady was born in Warren County, New York, probably in 1823. As a youth, the future photographer suffered from a "violent inflammation of the eyes" and would have vision problems lifelong. Perhaps this caused him to value vision even more than most people do. He was, in any case, about twelve years old in 1835 when he traveled to Albany and Saratoga for treatment of his ailing eyes, and during this trip he probably met the artist William Page. Some four years later, he sought employment in New York City—perhaps as a department store clerk—and was befriended by Samuel F. B. Morse, at the time a painter of note though soon to earn more fame and greater fortune as the inventor of the telegraph. He also made a friend of Samuel P. Avery, a prominent art dealer.

By 1843, Brady had set up as a maker of jewelry cases, with a shop at 164 Fulton Street in Lower Manhattan, and soon specialized in turning out custom cases to hold treasured daguerreotypes. By the following year, influenced by Page, Morse, and Avery, Brady opened a "Daguerrean Miniature Gallery" at 205–207 Broadway, corner of Fulton Street, then entered his own daguerreotypes in the annual fair of the American Institute, winning with them the coveted rank of "premium," the highest seal of approval the Institute could confer. This encouraged him in 1845 to begin making (as well as collecting from others) daguerreotype portraits of American men and women of prominence. He exhibited at American Institute again, and, again, collected top honors.

In 1846, Brady made a series of daguerreotypes of convicted criminals to be engraved for reproduction in *Rationale of Crime*, a book on phrenology by Marmaduke Sampson. In October, Brady for a third time received "premium" distinction from the American Institute, and the following month *Rationale of Crime* was published, with engravings after his daguerreotype originals. The book and the illustrations were very well received, but Brady seems to have made a deliberate decision not to pursue the use of photography to further document humanity's deviants and degenerates. He was determined instead to dedicate himself to creating a gallery of the noblest and most successful. By 1849, he had established studios in New York as well as Washington, strategic locations for drawing the nation's most distinguished personages to sit for him.

And sit they did. By 1850, photography was a growth industry in the United States. One observer in New York City this year counted seventy-one "rooms" (as photographic studios were often called) in the city, and within three years the *New York Tribune* counted one hundred, further estimating that, nationally, the photographic industry employed as many as seventeen thousand men and women and produced some three million images yearly. In these early boom times, Brady was a great success, attracting the likes of Daniel Webster; Jefferson Davis, future president of the Confederacy; the distinguished tragedian Edwin Forrest; the novelist James Fenimore Cooper; the "Great Compromiser" Henry Clay; Henry James Sr. and his young son, the future novelist Henry James Jr.; New York Tribune publisher Horace Greeley; President Zachary Taylor and his entire cabinet; John C. Calhoun, theorist of nullification and secession; future secretary of state William H. Seward; the U.S. Army's superannuated senior general, Winfield Scott; President James Buchanan; future Confederate vice president Judah P. Benjamin; abolitionist Senator Thaddeus Stevens; and many others. Abraham Lincoln sat for Brady a number of times, as did members of his family. Lincoln went so far as to credit an 1860 Brady portrait with having helped him to secure the Republican nomination for president.

As Brady developed his business and earned national renown through his New York and Washington galleries as well as various publications, he began working with wet-plate photography in addition to daguerreotypes, creating what he dubbed "Brady Imperials," impressive enlargements made from wet-plate negatives, including, in 1857, "a group of three full-length life-size [prints] on paper five feet by seven," which were, according to the reviewer for the *Photographic and Fine Art Journal*, "as remarkable for [their] excellence in color, tone and detail, as [for their] size."

In 1856, Brady's fame and achievement prompted Alexander Gardner to immigrate to America from Scotland and seek employment with the master. A great early photographer in his own right, Gardner would prove the most prolific and important of Brady's "operatives." Modern viewers of the work that emerged from the Brady studios sometimes accuse Brady of

ABOVE: *Mathew Brady photographed as many would see him on and around the battlefields, just a day after his escape from the advancing Confederate forces at Bull Run.*

BELOW: *Vain and rash, Judson Kilpatrick wanted nothing but the best for himself. That's why he left the battlefield and went to a Brady studio to sit for a portrait that was made in 1863 or later. He must have chafed at the meticulous way in which the photographer arranged his pose, but once the camera was ready to be used the brigadier sat perfectly still for several seconds.*

taking credit for the work of his operatives, especially Gardner. In fact, Brady did no such thing. While it is true that the photographs of everyone who worked for Brady, including Gardner, were generally identified with the inscription "Photo by Brady"—which became one of the most familiar trademarks of the late 1850s and the Civil War period—Brady made no secret of employing a staff of photographers and generally billed himself as the man who made the assignments and presided over the galleries. He did visit a number of battlefields, and he can be seen in various battlefield photographs—his flowing duster, distinctive profile accented by the pointed "imperial" beard fashionable during the period, and his broad-brimmed straw hat were conspicuous trademarks—but Gardner and others certainly took more "Brady" photographs than Brady himself did. Increasingly as the years went by, Brady was the entrepreneur, who left much of the fieldwork, the actual photography, to others. This may have been due as much to failing eyesight as to personal preference.

Whatever the motives for the marked division of authorship that characterized the Brady studio's Civil War photographs, historians of photography have seen a key aesthetic difference between photographs known or believed to be Brady's and those known or believed to be Gardner's. Brady favored heroic, even quasi-mythic images of officers and men grouped and posed in the field, whereas Gardner was drawn to the more naked reality of documentation. It is generally agreed that all of the post-combat photographs of battlefields that show the bodies of the slain are the work of the Scotsman. Yet even in these ghastly images, Gardner was rarely the totally pure and objective documentarian. Look closely at the battlefield images in this book. Few really suggest the chaos of combat. In most, the dead are arrayed as if they had fallen in perfect order of rank and file. Almost certainly, the photographer and his assistants arranged them before the shutter was opened and the exposure made. Nevertheless, the difference between Brady and Gardner remains striking and suggests that the impetus of Brady's prewar vocation as a portraitist and his ambition to collect images of the most important figures of his time never really deserted him. Whether in the studio or the field, the people before his lens were to be portrayed as heroic in their very presence.

While historians and critics sometimes argue over the actual authorship of various photos "by Brady," no one disputes the fact that it was Brady's idea to cover the war in the first place. In 1891, he recounted to an interviewer, G. A. Townsend, that his wife as well as his "most

BELOW: *Pedestrians and riders along Broadway in 1853 could hardly have failed to be impressed at the height of Brady's new studio and gallery. It towered upward for four full stories.*

INSET: *By the time* The Photographic Art Journal *decided to publish an engraved likeness of the nation's best-known photographer, Brady had become an expensively dressed* dandy. *However, he did not attempt to wear clothing of this sort when he began his life-consuming task of photographing the Union side of the Civil War.*

RIGHT: *As depicted by graver A. Berghaus, walls of the spacious Brady gallery on Broadway were lined with portraits of notables.*

conservative friends had looked unfavorably upon this departure from commercial business to pictorial war correspondence." Nevertheless, Brady explained to Townsend, "I felt that I had to go. A spirit in my feet said 'Go,' and I went." Because of the esteem in which President Lincoln and many high-ranking Union officers held Brady—all had sat for him—he had no difficulty obtaining passes for himself and his band of photographers to come and go freely with the army in the field.

His initial ambition was to photograph the First Battle of Bull Run on July 21, 1861, but he was driven off the field—along with a stunned and demoralized Union army—before he could capture anything very meaningful. In the spring of 1862, Gardner left Brady's employ to work for the publicity-conscious Major General George B. McClellan as the official photographer of the Army of the Potomac. By the fall of that year, various battlefield images began to appear in *Harper's Weekly*, all credited to Brady, including pictures of Antietam that were certainly the work of Gardner. Throughout the war, even after Gardner opened his own studio late in 1862, a great many war-related photographs would be indiscriminately credited to Brady, whose renown rose steadily, even as his finances began to decline, edging more and more certainly toward total collapse.

In the end, covering the Civil War proved to be of monumental historical importance, but bad business. On September 7, 1864, in an effort to stave off bankruptcy, Brady sold half his Washington gallery to James Gibson, the gallery manager, for $10,000, half in cash, the rest in notes. In May 1865, *Harper's Weekly* published a moving series of engravings based on Brady's full photographic coverage of President Lincoln's funeral procession, and in January of the following year, Brady tried unsuccessfully to persuade the New-York Historical Society to purchase all of his war views and war-related portraits for the modest sum of $30,000. The deal, which looked promising, suddenly fell through, and on June 26, 1868, Brady filed suit against James Gibson over the bankruptcy of the Washington gallery they jointly owned. When the gallery was sold at auction the next month, Brady managed to scrape together the $7,600 necessary to buy it back.

During the late 1860s and early 1870s, Mathew Brady continued to enjoy renown as a photographer and gallery owner, but his financial credit continued to erode, and on January 30, 1873, the District Court of the United States for the Southern District of New York declared him bankrupt. Left with nothing but his photographic collection, he turned to Congress, seeking to sell it all for a low six-figure sum. In March 1875, after dithering for two years, Congress offered Brady a mere $25,000 for clear title to all of his negatives and prints. It was barely sufficient to discharge his debts and secure his release from bankruptcy, leaving Mathew Brady with very little. His New York studios were gone, and his Washington studio was burdened by a heavy mortgage.

Thanks to a continued demand from magazine editors for his work, Brady kept his head above water, even as his eyesight and health declined. The years passed heavily, and in April 1895, Brady, now

seventy-three years old, was struck by a horsecar on a Washington street and suffered a badly fractured leg. The bones failed to knit, and the injury never healed. By the end of the year, he was hospitalized, apparently with kidney failure, and, on January 16, 1896, Mathew Brady died in New York's Presbyterian Hospital.

Brady died broke, but hardly forgotten. During the war, the New York 7th Regiment had made him an honorary member, and now the New York Seventh Regiment Veterans Association, together with art dealer Samuel Avery and a few other friends, paid for his funeral.

Thanks to the congressional purchase, the great majority of the photographs Brady either made himself, commissioned, collected, or controlled are held and curated by the Library of Congress and are available to the public as part of the great American heritage. They draw us—and will continue to draw the generations that follow us—almost as near to the Civil War as they had drawn the generation that actually lived through that war. They are the bitter, beautiful, heroic, horrific, and enduring graphic legacy of that war, the first significant body of images recording an American conflict.

There would be more—more wars, more pictures—and with each war, the technology of photography, then of filmmaking and television, would develop and improve, making the images more numerous, detailed, extensive, immediate, and complete, but never more compelling, never more terribly fascinating.

Alan Axelrod

RIGHT: *Mathew Brady's pursuit of a photo documentary of the Civil War left the once-wealthy daguerrotypist flat broke. This 1889 portrait by L. C. Handy reveals a weary man whose face and eyes lack the eager sparkle that marked those of the photographer who trudged from one battlefield to another for four years to record the tragedy of war.*

CIVILIAN
AND MILITARY LEADERS

"It is well that war is so terrible, or we shall grow too fond of it."
Robert E. Lee, Fredericksburg, 1862

Mathew Brady won an international reputation and amassed a small fortune by specializing in portraits of powerful civilians. He made no secret of the fact that he opened a Washington studio primarily to get ready access to national leaders. Since he and Alexander Gardner plus their aides had instant access to the Lincoln White House, it is appropriate that his collection includes a large gallery of politicians and high-ranking military personnel.

Portraits of persons who today would be described as "beltway insiders" covered a substantial segment of the wall space in his Broadway gallery. Some who adorned its walls were rich and famous during 1840-60, but are forgotten today; many others will never be forgotten.

Focus of cameras upon civilians other than the president plus his cabinet members and aides all but ended after secessionists fired upon Fort Sumter in April, 1861. In postwar years he decided, however, to photograph U.S. members of an international commission established to settle the "the Alabama claims."

Brady's collection of glass negatives that hold images of high-ranking Union officers has no parallel in scope or in composition. Unfortunately, he rarely recorded names of subordinates to his principal subject and sometimes failed to jot a notation concerning the date or period when an individual or group photo was made. He rarely turned his attention to a Confederate or an ex-Confederate. When he did, however, he focused his camera upon a man of surpassing importance and depicted his subject in the best possible manner.

Only a very small fraction of the Brady collection of photographs of notable military leaders is included here. Dozens of other highly important leaders willingly "froze" for the camera. Those whose portraits, individual or group, appear here provide an unduplicated look at men who laid their lives on the line for the sake of the Union.

Detective Alan Pinkerton (left), who dodged cameras and assumed a false identity in order to penetrate Rebel lines, appears anything but relaxed as he poses with his leader. Perhaps it was because he had helped Brady gain permission to go to battlefields that he posed for him – probably reluctantly. Gen. John A. McClernand, of Kentucky, a long time favorite of Lincoln, was a vexatious "thorn in the flesh" to U.S. Grant for two years, beginning in February, 1862.

LEFT: *Early in the "accidental presidency" of Andrew Johnson, it became clear that he and members of Congress would clash over Reconstruction of the defeated South. After a series of quarrels, the House of Representatives voted to launch impeachment proceedings. A Brady photo of the managers of the impeachment proceedings and trial shows two former military officers and five prominent political leaders. Seated are former Gen. Benjamin F. Butler (a distinguished Massachusetts attorney), Thaddeus Stevens of Pennsylvania, Thomas Williams of Pennsylvania, and John A. Bingham of Ohio. Standing behind them are: James F. Wilson of Iowa, George S. Bothwell of Massachusetts, and former Gen. John A. ("Blackjack") Logan of Illinois.*

RIGHT: *Gen. George B. McClellan (right of center, wearing sash) took command of all Federal forces after the Bull Run debacle. Handsome, talented, and ambitious, he won the hearts of staff officers shown here plus the adulation of tens of thousands of troops. His staff included two members of the French nobility. They were the Prince de Joinville (wearing hat, third from right in photo) and the Comte de Paris (to his left). These foreign observers stayed with McClellan for months, and both saw combat.*

RIGHT: *Godfrey Wetzel (seated, center) was a talented military engineer from Ohio. He helped plan defenses of Cincinnati and Washington, then became Benjamin F. Butler's chief engineer. Fifteen staff officers, not all of whom have been identified, posed with him no earlier than September or October, 1862. Wetzel didn't get his single-star shoulder straps until August 29, 1862, and it took weeks to organize his staff.*

LEFT: *Generals usually posed alone or with a group of staff officers. Brady managed to capture four general officers, with no aides. Harvard graduate Francis Barlow (left) enlisted as a private, was severely wounded at Antietam, and soon afterward became a brigadier. He still sports the checked "hickory shirt" worn by many enlisted men. Winfield Scott Hancock (seated) became a general officer in September, 1861, and fought throughout the war with distinction. John Gibbon of Pennsylvania, standing behind Hancock, had three brothers in gray uniforms; nevertheless, he was made a brigadier in May, 1862. David B. Barney, of Alabama (right), became a major general in May, 1863. This photo was made some time after the spring of that year.*

RIGHT: *Brigadier General Edwin V Sumner, easily distinguished by his white beard, posed with seven staff officers before the Marshall house at Warranton, Virginia. Lt. Samuel S. Sumner, standing close to him, was his son.*

RIGHT: *Brigadier General Joseph "Fighting Joe" Hooker proudly posed with a white horse he rarely rode in combat – the white animal made a great target for Rebel sharpshooters. Horseman though he was, Hooker couldn't persuade "Whitey" to keep his tail still for four seconds.*

LEFT: *Despite British neutrality laws, the Confederate commerce raider C.S.S.* Alabama *and other raiders emerged from British shipyards during the Civil War. After the war, a special commission was authorized to settle with Britain "the Alabama claims." In 1872 the international tribunal awarded the United States $15,500,000 in gold. For its part, Britain was paid $1,929,819 for damages suffered by her subjects.*

LEFT: *Winfield Scott Hancock turned down command of the Army of the Potomac because he couldn't get Washington to give him a free hand. He saw the command go to George G. Meade after midnight on June 28, 1863 – only hours before Gettysburg would become one of the world's best-known battlefields. A major general, Hancock had a decisive role in persuading Meade to make Seminary Ridge the strategic center of the Federal line in that battle.*

RIGHT: *Swashbuckling Jeb Stuart reached the Gettysburg battleground many hours behind schedule, thereby denying Lee of intelligence he badly needed. Some theorists believe that if he hadn't been making another mad dash around a huge Federal force, the outcome at Gettysburg might have been different. Reaching the battlefield late on the second day of fighting, Stuart contributed little to the Confederate effort.*

LEFT: *District of Columbia native David Hunter became a major general soon after Bull Run. Sent to Hilton Head, South Carolina, to command the military Department of the South, he issued orders liberating all slaves in the department. Lincoln forced the repeal of this early "emancipation proclamation," but Hunter was not abashed. He organized three regiments of blacks – and won Congressional approval for this move. After the war, he accompanied the body of his slain president on the long rail journey to Springfield, then returned to the capital to preside over the commission that tried the accused conspirators.*

RIGHT: *Even after he had become a Union major general in April, 1862, many men commanded by Virginia native George H. Thomas derided him as "Old Slow Trot." He lost that nickname at Chickamauga, where his firm stand prevented a rout of the Union forces. After that, he became widely known as "The Rock of Chickamauga" and snide quips about him came to a halt.*

RIGHT: *General Thomas L. Crittenden of Kentucky was close to the bottom of the list of efficient Union commanders. Son of the powerful senator who had proposed an eleventh-hour reconciliation between North and South (the "Crittenden Compromise"), he hung his head with shame when he learned that his brother, George, had become a Confederate brigadier. Though the two men from the Bluegrass State never met in combat, they symbolized the fashion in which the North/South struggle pitted "brother against brother."*

LEFT: *Marsena Patrick of New York State fought in numerous battles before becoming provost marshal of the Army of the Potomac. He performed well in an unpopular job, which entailed keeping thousands of unruly men in order.*

RIGHT: *With a show-down battle looming in Pennsylvania, the colorful 23-year-old George Armstrong Custer was jumped past most of his peers and made a brigadier by George. G. Meade. After Gettysburg, Custer fought in numerous other battles. Aside from his Civil War service, he is best known for his defeat and death at the Little Bighorn River on June 25, 1876. This is a postwar photograph, since Custer didn't display the insignia of a major general until after April 15, 1865.*

LEFT: *New Yorker Philip H. Sheridan's spotty record at West Point relegated him to minor assignments when war broke out. Finally given a command as a cavalry colonel, he had to wear an infantry captain's uniform because he had nothing else. Grant ultimately selected him to head the cavalry corps of the Army of the Potomac. His forces defeated those of Jeb Stuart at Yellow Tavern, where the legendary Confederate was killed. It was long axiomatic on both sides that Rebel riders always trounced their opponents. Sheridan smashed that myth at Cedar Creek, where he turned a sure Federal defeat into a victory.*

RIGHT: By 1864, Brady and/or his operatives had taken so many photos of the war-time president that he became widely known as "Lincoln's photographer."

LEFT: *Having been named a Confederate commissioner to France, James M. Mason set out to cross the Atlantic Ocean on the Royal Mail Steamer* Trent *late in 1861. The vessel was stopped by the U.S.S.* San Jacinto *on November 8 and Mason was taken aboard the warship under arrest. Lincoln initially applauded the actions of Capt. James Wilkes of the U.S. Navy. Soon, however, Britain took serious steps toward entering the North American fray. When it was learned that 15,000 of Her Majesty's best soldiers were headed toward Canada, Mason was hastily released and a formal apology was sent to London.*

LEFT: *Major General Ambrose Everett Burnside will forever be remembered for his flamboyant mutton-chop whiskers, which came to be called "burnsides," eventually changed to "sideburns." Burnside's Civil War career was marked by a few successes (for example, securing a Union foothold on the North Carolina coast for future penetrations of the Confederate interior), and even more failures, including senseless and costly attacks at Fredericksburg in December 1862, an inept mud-bound winter campaign in Virginia, and a bungled attack on the Crater at Petersburg late in the war.*

LEFT: *Confederate Tennessee was badly divided during much of the war, with Unionists predominating at her eastern tip. Appointed military governor of the state in 1862, Andrew Johnson organized and led a faction loyal to Washington and for two years served as a brigadier. In 1864 he was rewarded by being named Lincoln's running mate. Upon Lincoln's assassination, he became chief executive and was the first to be impeached, but was not convicted.*

RIGHT: *Hawk-faced William H. Seward of New York was nationally known as "Mr. Republican" in 1860. When he lost the nomination for the presidency to Lincoln, he accepted an offer to become secretary of state in the first Republican administration. He almost certainly thought that he would make all major decisions, but soon found that the gangling chief executive had a mind of his own. He remained in Lincoln's cabinet and served effectively throughout the war.*

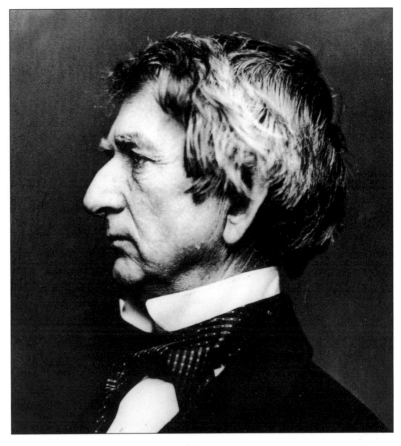

RIGHT: *Alexander H. Stephens of Georgia opposed secession, yet when his state left the Union, he accepted the vice-presidency of the Confederate States. Because he and Jefferson Davis seldom agreed on any subject, he spent little time in Richmond. In cooperation with northern proponents of peace, he tried without success to bring contending sides together at Hampton Roads, Virginia. Many authorities say that the peace conference failed because of the slavery issue. In truth, the insuperable difficulty was Lincoln's demand for unconditional surrender on the part of the South.*

COMPANIES
AND REGIMENTS

"The entire garrison of 13,000 men with their well-kept equipment, their new uniforms, and beautiful banners 'surrendered' to Jackson's gaunt and ragged soldiers...."

An officer with Lee's army, following events at Harpers Ferry, September 15, 1862

Since the size of a company varied from about 50 to a maximum of 100 men, it was the easiest unit to form. Many a zealous member of a community successfully set out to "raise a company," of which he expected to be elected captain.

Once formed, the company – North and South – was normally divided into four squads, each led by a sergeant or a corporal. For purposes of record, a company was assigned an identifying letter so that it became, for example,

Company F, 4th Michigan (infantry).

Members of many companies gave their units colorful names by which they came to be known throughout their regiments. These unofficial names rarely appear in military orders, dispatches, or reports but sprinkle pages of thousands of letters and diaries.

The regiment, whose normal maximum strength was 10 companies, was the basic organizational unit of southern and northern military forces. No other aspect of the war so clearly demonstrates the enormous power of the states' rights movement in the North as well as in the South. Governors selected the colonels who led regiments of men from their state. Each regiment protected its state identity fiercely, and even after becoming decimated from combat resisted "amalgamation" with another regiment in order to form a new unit of regulation size.

Life within a regiment was so cohesive and all-important that hundreds of regimental histories are available. Only a handful of company histories have been issued.

Throughout this volume, infantry regiments are identified simply by their numbers and their states – such as 9th Indiana. If a regiment is an artillery, cavalry, or engineering unit, it is so designated.

Only a few members of the 9th Indiana responded when told to "Fall out to get yer picture taken." Unlike many formal regimental photos, this one shows men wearing anything they wished. Still, the motley band stacked a few muskets so they'd look "soldier like." Comfortable in their winter camp, they had become accustomed to lax discipline. Many of them must have grumbled when an officer appeared at the right end of their line in the photo and ordered them to "dress it" before the shutter clicked.

LEFT: *A few officers of the U.S. Army's 5th Cavalry show no interest in the map one of them pulled out on request. Under an arbitrary but rigid system, military units were listed alphabetically by states. Within a state list cavalry regiments were listed first. Heavy and light artillery followed, then came engineers. Sharpshooters followed engineers in state lists that had such units. Infantry units were at the tail ends of all lists.*

RIGHT: *Four members of the U.S. Army's 4th Infantry, with their colonel at left in the photo. Washington decided to keep the U.S. Army intact, rather than disperse its members throughout volunteer units. In the opinion of foreign analysts, this was a serious mistake – a few men of experience could quickly have prepared green troops to fight. As it was, specialists such as are shown here had little or no contact with volunteers.*

BELOW: *Professional soldiers, most of whom had extensive experience, from Co. D., U.S. Army, 4th Infantry. The officer at the right in the photo is smoking, probably having gotten a little tobacco by illicit trading with the enemy. Far the most common items swapped between men of the North and the South were coffee and tobacco.*

RIGHT: *Four majors and lieutenant colonels of the U.S. Army's 4th Infantry. Two officers of this unit showed up in civilian clothing, minus swords and wearing jaunty hats. Stationed in California in January, 1861, this unit was brought to Washington to help defend the capital. It took part in at least three dosen battles, but only two officers and 58 enlisted men were killed in action. Disease took the lives of one officer and 61 enlisted men.*

ABOVE: *Tent No. 8, Company F, 4th Michigan. Some of these fellows had managed to get their hands on smokes. The tent in which they slept and sometimes lived was designed to hold a maximum of four men. Organized at Adrian, the regiment was mustered in a month prior to Bull Run. Its members served for four years plus ten days.*

RIGHT: *Lt. Parker, who was commissary officer of the 4th Michigan, brought along three of his helpers when asked to pose for the camera. Revolvers, which were comparatively rare and expensive, were issued to enlisted members of cavalry and artillery units, but not to infantry men. Those infantry soldiers who had them bought them with their own money. The black crouching at left in the photo (typical position at which these men appear) may have been a contraband who had been pressed into service, but it's equally possible that he was Parker's body servant.*

LEFT: *Members of the 21st Michigan were detailed for engineer duty late in 1863. During more than six months, when they built bridges, storehouses, and other structures, they spent their spare time putting up semi-permanent cottages for use as headquarters. A symbolic apple that hung from the center of each cottage gave these men a sense of "being at home," even though they were far away.*

LEFT: *Men of an unidentified company of the 21st Michigan fell out of winter camp in order to be photographed with their captain and their drummer. Organized at Iona and Grand Rapids, the regiment was ordered to Louisville, Kentucky, and left the state on September 9. Most of their 32 months of service was spent in the western theater, where they took part in most major battles.*

BELOW: *The "spit and polish" that marked men of the 21st Michigan disappeared long before they reached Savannah, Georgia, on Sherman's March to the Sea. Men of this regiment then marched through both Carolinas and thence to Washington by way of Richmond. Sore-footed as they were, they proudly took part in the Grand Review of Union troops on May 24, 1865.*

LEFT: *Four officers of the 15th New York Engineers did their best to look comfortably relaxed before the camera. They probably didn't realise that in their hurry they had hung their regimental banner backward before lounging on deluxe folding chairs. The unidentified officer at the right holds a boot hook or a riding crop.*

LEFT: *With a bit of their wash hanging on a line, a few officers of the 16th Pennsylvania Cavalry tried to look both soldierly and casual. The booted fellow at the left in the picture was showing off; he wouldn't have been smoking a pipe while holding a cigar. The contraband or the body servant on the ground at the right probably sneaked into view an instant before the shutter clicked.*

RIGHT: *Officers of the 164th New York posed on a breezy day. Every man wore a regulation uniform, and dress swords were prominently displayed. Fuzzy limbs of trees behind them show that the wind refused to die down for a mere four seconds.*

RIGHT: *Some of the members of an unidentified company of the 170th New York gathered on a hillside for this photo. As usual, their drummer is at the left in the picture. Fourth in a string of units popularly known as the "Corcoran Legion," they were mustered in when war had been raging for more than a year. Despite its relative short term of service, the regiment lost 10 officers and 119 enlisted men in combat. Two officers and 96 enlisted men died of disease during their three-year hitch.*

RIGHT: *Members of an unidentified regiment probably didn't turn out specially for this photograph; the camera was ready as they finished dressing their line. Fuzziness of the flag indicates that a brisk wind was blowing on this snowy day.*

BELOW: *A few officers of the 139th Pennsylvania, including an unidentified brigadier at the right, willingly posed. Organized at Pittsburgh when the shooting war was 16 months old, men of this unit helped to bury the dead after Second Bull Run. They fought at Antietam and Fredericksburg and took part in Burnside's disastrous "mud march" before again being in combat at Chancellorsville and Gettysburg. After five months in the siege of Petersburg, they helped pursue the Army of Northern Virginia to Appomattox Court House.*

RIGHT: *Members of an unidentified infantry company had spent many hours giving their camp headquarters a distinctive look.*

DRESS AND INSIGNIA

"Clothes really do make the man; that's why I wear velvet bought with my own money."

Brigadier General George Armstrong Custer

When armed conflict began, lack of uniformity in dress of troops was a major problem, especially among Federal forces. Many men who had gladly agreed to fight for the Union for 90 days showed up at Bull Run in uniforms of various shades of gray. This inevitably led to numerous instances in which comrades fired upon comrades. Militia units in widely varied outfits fought in early conflicts. Zouaves, who imagined that they had fashioned uniforms that would be familiar in the Middle East, fought on both sides and gave enemies bright targets at which to shoot.

Some of the confusion was eliminated by the end of 1861, but the problems created by color of dress were never fully resolved. Many Rebel units didn't have gray, so they fought in what they often termed "butternut" uniforms – essentially, civilian clothing. Close to the end of the war, North Carolina textile mills turned out a big batch of Confederate uniforms before taking care that they had suitable dyes on hand. When no gray could be found, these were dyed blue – and shipped off for use by Confederate units.

On both sides, insignia was an all-important concern. It was much easier to see buttons on the front of an officer's uniform jacket or his sleeve than to get a good look at the shoulder straps he wore. Brady and his operatives were downright unconcerned about keeping exact records concerning dates, ranks, and names of their subjects. In many instances, insignia help to fill in blanks. An officer's rank can often be determined at a glance, and his rank can be used to determine whether a photo was taken before or after a change in rank.

Though widely overlooked, dress and insignia constitute a fascinating window into the war.

Throughout both North and South, citizens of towns and counties took great pride in providing members of militia units with unusual and distinctive uniforms. Men of the 1st Vermont Cavalry left Burlington for Washington in November, 1861. These proud fellows wouldn't have been caught dead in a regulation-issue Federal uniform. Sgt. Patrick Hogan was so colorful that his photo was snapped soon after he and his gaudily bedecked comrades reached the capital.

LEFT: *When lounging around camp, men were permitted to wear whatever they pleased, including a "hickory shirt," such as that of Pvt. Emory Eugene of the 4th Michigan. When preparing to face the camera, he added to his look of bravado by sticking a huge non-regulation Bowie knife in his belt. Eugene was not wholly unconventional, however. Despite his dress, he stuck the customary right hand inside his outer garment.*

BELOW: *Brigadier General George Armstrong Custer, left, was outranked when he posed with Alfred Pleasonton, a major general. No one ever accused the ringlet-dangling cavalry*

RIGHT: *At the outbreak of war, Hiram Berdan of New York was widely considered to be the best marksman with a rifle on the North American continent. He suggested that it would be wise to organise a regiment of sharpshooters, and was promptly made its colonel. Many of the men who flocked to fight under his command brought their own fine rifles, some of which were equipped with telescopic sights. His buttons silently proclaim his rank, but he probably never went into combat wearing white gauntlets and an elaborate sash.*

commander of being out-dressed, though. Here his sleeves are lavishly bedecked with the gold braid that men of his command derided – behind his back – as "chicken guts."

LEFT: *Some commanders, among whom U. S. Grant was conspicuous, seemed to care nothing about dress. Oral tradition has it that a private in his command encountered him in a uniform identical to his, and addressed him as a peer. In this delightful shot Grant's three shoulder-strap stars identify him as the only lieutenant general in blue, but the three-button pattern on his uniform jacket is that of a major general.*

RIGHT: *Like most high-ranking officers, William T. Sherman rarely wore gloves. It is difficult, however, to tell whether the white band at the end of his left arm is his shirt cuff or the white arm band all U.S. officers were required to wear during a six-month period following the assassination of Lincoln. If it is the mourning band, then we know the photograph dates from after April 15, 1865.*

LEFT: *Buttons arranged in patterns of three instantly informed every military man that Edward M. McCook had reached the rank of major general. In his case, the rank was brevet (honorary) only, conferred postwar by the U.S. Congress. McCook's display of buttons therefore says this photo was made after 1865.*

LEFT: *The fife and drum corps of an unidentified regiment. All drummers had distinctive white support straps that made them instantly recognizable.*

LEFT: *John S. Mosby had a commission as a Confederate colonel, but operated as leader of a band of partisan rangers. The three stars on his collar mark his rank as colonel, as does the arrangement of buttons on his jacket. The blue colonel's uniform at his feet may have been worn on a raid in which he disguised himself as an officer of enemy forces.*

RIGHT: *C.S. Col. M. S. Stokes donned an official uniform for this studio portrait with elaborately ornamented sleeves. Buttons, worn in pairs, are identical to those of a Rebel major general.*

LEFT: *C.S. Major General John B. Gordon, fought with distinction throughout the war. If only the buttons on his jacket were visible, he might be taken for a colonel. Three stars encircled by laurel leaves on each side of his collar indicate that he is a general officer.*

BELOW: *Confederate naval officers were offered considerable latitude in dress and insignia. For this portrait, Capt. John Pemberton put on epaulets – mandatory for dress parades – plus white gloves. His sleeves display two comparatively wide stripes, but the pattern of his buttons is not distinguishable from that of much higher officers. Someone wrote his name on the back of the negative; otherwise he might have been listed as "unidentified."*

ABOVE: *Before the war, George E. Pickett had been a successful Virginia attorney. At Gettysburg his name became forever linked with the heroic but ill-fated "Pickett's Charge" – an action actually ordered by Robert E. Lee. When Pickett became a major general late in 1862, Rebels weren't yet experiencing severe shortages of all essentials. He therefore wore the usual laurel-wreathed stars on his collar plus elaborate arm braid – and adopted the three-button pattern that had been set by Federal major generals.*

RIGHT: *The Union navy's David D. Porter went to sea at age nine. His first significant Civil War victory came at the capture of New Orleans. For this he was made an acting rear admiral. Wearing buttons of that rank, he donned gold epaulets for a studio portrait in which he took care to display his decorated belt and three gold arm bands surmounted by a star. In comparative flamboyance, his arm bands fall short of those displayed by General George A. Custer, but ordinary seamen under his command nevertheless joked about his display of "chicken guts."*

LEFT: *U.S. Rear Admiral Andrew H. Foote's gold bands on his sleeves make his rank instantly recognizable, even though the insignia on his shoulder straps is not fully visible in the photograph. He received his high rank plus the Thanks of Congress for his crucial role in the first significant Federal naval victory, at Fort Donaldson on Tennessee's Cumberland River.*

CAMP LIFE

"Drills and parades were great fun –
until secessionists attacked us in the streets of Baltimore."
A sergeant in 6th Massachusetts, made up of 90-day volunteers

Every regiment spent some time in a temporary or permanent camp.
When men flocked to Washington in response to Lincoln's first call for 75,000
volunteers, most or all of them were assigned to camps where they spent
weeks drilling and learning to use their weapons. Many of these men left
camp for Bull Run, and once the battle was over went home.

Some elite regiments, South and North, didn't enjoy a stay in a permanent
camp during the entire war, however. They fought, marched to new destinations,
fought again, and then marched to a new point of contact with the enemy. Other
regiments, whose members initially moaned that they were being treated unfairly,
were assigned to guard railroads, bridges, and other vital points. Once the war got
well under way, the majority of men in these regiments rejoiced at their good
luck. Thousands of men in such units never saw combat.

Temporary camps, sometimes thrown up en route to a battle, gave some shelter
from wind and rain but little else. Many such camps were made up of hundreds of
"A," tents, each of which held up to twice the number of men for which they were
designed. When tents were struck, men of a camp marched until ordered to
stop, then threw up another temporary camp.

Permanent and semi-permanent camps were likely to be dotted with wooden
structures that were reasonably comfortable. Men of some units spent days erecting
decorative arches and other structures by which they signified their pride in their
regiment. When a permanent camp was evacuated, these decorative structures
were often left standing.

Regardless of how little provision was made for camp life among enlisted men, officers usually fared
well. Their quarters were sturdier and much less crowded than those of the enlistees. If they became
bored sitting around their own shelter, they could always lounge at a headquarters building. These
officers of an unidentified unit, who were photographed very early in the war, may not have seen
combat. Note the young African American, who is dressed in an outfit befitting a valet or orderly.

LEFT: *Camped near Alexandria, Virginia, for an extended period, men of the 44th New York devoted some of their idle time to letting passersby know the number of their unit and some of the engagements in which they had taken part. Since they fought at Mine Run early in the winter of 1863, they must have gone into camp soon after this battle.*

RIGHT: *A show of cold steel was widely believed to throw fear into the hearts of enemies; hence men on both sides typically drilled with bayonets attached to the tips of their hand weapons. When encamped, a regiment might spend several hours a day in a series of bayonet drills*

LEFT: *Viewed from the rear, the camp of the 40th New York near Alexandria, Virginia, was a model of tidiness as well as beauty. Since this photo was made from a considerable distance in order to capture the entire camp, the town of Alexandria shows up clearly in the background.*

LEFT: *In many camps, drills and parades took up at least half of a fellow's time. Officers figured that unless men of a company could properly dress their line, they'd be useless in battles that were often fought in formal European fashion, one line of troops standing and firing at the opposing line. Each of the six big Sibley tents was designed to accommodate at least a dozen men. Henry H. Sibley developed this tent – modified from the teepee of the Plains Indians – during prewar years as an Indian fighter.*

RIGHT: *To enlisted men, hours of relaxation often seemed entirely too few. As soon as they were dismissed, many fellows shucked their uniforms and raced to start a card game.*

RIGHT: **Horseplay was an integral part of camp life. With comrades watching, two men square off with swords borrowed from officers. Taking no chances, the fellow at the right is ready to brandish a pistol if his buddy proves more adept with steel. The African-American soldier seen in this photograph was doubtless an orderly or laborer, since the army was strictly segregated.**

LEFT: *In camps that were occupied for only a night or two, a sutler's wagon rolled behind the troops. As soon as a march halted, the proprietor was ready to sell sought-after items at high prices. In permanent camps, the regimental sutler often operated out of a sturdy place that became a favorite spot at which men loafed and lounged. The presence of their colonel has not inhibited these fellows, one of whom fondles a huge jug and another entertains with a fife - or pokes fun at the officer behind his back!*

LEFT: *In short-term camps, all company kitchens were likely to be tents. Not so in the case of a company whose men knew they would be at a specific locality for weeks or months. With 60 to 100 men having several hours a day of free time, it was easy to get a sturdy company kitchen built. Only one "contraband" (African-American orderly or servant) is shown in this photograph of men who were asked to pose with some of their utensils in hand.*

LEFT: *Though the commissary department of a fighting unit specialized in hard tack, its staff could rely upon an occasional God-send brought back by a forage party. The dressed beef hanging under the tent would probably disappear after the next meal.*

RIGHT: *Supplies enough to last for weeks were to be stacked around or close to a permanent kitchen. Huge quantities of flour arrived in barrels. Frequently, a novel use was found for an empty barrel. Here one of them seems to have had its head and bottom knocked out in order to form an extension of the chimney.*

RIGHT: *Hay was one of the war's basic commodities. Many companies and regiments had piles of it. This one, attached to the Army of the Potomac, shows a fraction of the quantity used by this army in a single day. The smockwearer in the right foreground may be Mathew Brady.*

RIGHT: *Many companies and regiments owned portable outdoor stoves and took them wherever they went. These were a lot better than nothing in intervals when troops were on the move so constantly that they didn't establish camps and had no chance to throw up a cook tent. Even when cooking facilities of some sort were available, those men who managed to get their hands on coffee often boiled it in a can over an open fire.*

RIGHT: *Wherever camps sprang up, cook tents were present. Some were replaced by stout semi-permanent kitchens. As surely as a cook tent was spotted, an observer would see one or more black workers, escaped slaves treated by Federal forces as contraband of war. Huge numbers of African Americans were used as laborers long before any were accepted as soldiers.*

LEFT: *Officers and men frequently went for weeks or months without a bath. Yet nearly all semi-permanent and permanent camps had a few tubs in which clothing could be hand-washed – usually by contrabands.*

LEFT: *John Henry, as he was called by the men for whom he was a general-purpose servant, was a "camp treasure" in every sense of the word. Described as being unusually intelligent, he was given cast-off boots and a ragged colonel's uniform by those he served.*

LEFT: *When a company or regiment was stationed for more than a few days at a given spot, officers often turned a civilian's home into a headquarters building. When no suitable structure of this sort was available, enlisted men pitched in, cut trees, and built rough but sturdy headquarters buildings. This one was the handiwork of men of Company F, 11th Rhode Island, who camped for a period at Miners Hill, Virginia.*

RIGHT: *Except in permanent camps, shelter space was almost always scarce. This "A" tent was designed to hold four men, but it appears to have been the temporary home of at least seven soldiers of the 22nd New York. It's highly improbable that the two black servants at the rear right in the photo were permitted to sleep in this or any other tent.*

LEFT: *Religious services were conducted in camps at sporadic intervals. Here a priest conducts mass for the heavily Roman Catholic 69th New York State Militia. This three-month unit fought for the Union during three separate 90-day periods. When mustered out for the third time in October, 1864, the unit had experienced a highly unusual casualty rate. Typically, disease felled far more men than bullets did, but, in the 69th, only four enlisted men died from disease, while one officer and 44 enlisted men were killed or mortally wounded in combat. Three reasons for this anomaly are likely: (1) short-term service enabled sick men to get civilian medical treatment; (2) "battle fatigue" didn't hit men very hard during any 90-day period; (3) while they spent long intervals back home in New York, sick and dying men were replaced with healthy recruits.*

LEFT: *Construction of a winter camp was a major undertaking. Once hundreds of trees were felled and trimmed, their trunks were often supplemented with canvas, plus boards from the nearest sawmill. The draped wagon partially visible at the right may have been one of many that Brady equipped and sent into the field.*

BELOW: *Compared with tents, "cottages" in some winter camps were elegant. Brady or one of his operatives almost certainly instructed these happy fellows to vary their headgear as widely as possible and to bring along implements. The broom may have been used regularly, but a cottage with no chimney had little or no use for the axe that had been central to its construction.*

ABOVE: *When a building that was to be used in winter quarters was under construction, all of the manual labor was done by enlisted men – who were not paid for their extra service. Almost always, mounted officers served as superintendents of construction. Here, several appear to have converged when word was spread that a photograph would be made. Buttons on his uniform say that the officer in center front was a brigadier – and men of this rank seldom devoted time to routine construction jobs.*

THE BATTLEFIELDS

"It was never my fortune to witness a more bloody, dismal battlefield."

Major General Joseph Hooker, on Antietam

Brady and his operatives photographed many a battleground, but no battles. Equipment of the day wasn't capable of freezing action – and men in the middle of a fight never, never, attempted to remain still for four seconds in order to be photographed.

Having witnessed a resounding Federal defeat, Matthew Brady probably returned from Bull Run full of questions. He knew that the war was likely to be much longer and bloodier than the conflict promised by Lincoln. Yet he had no yardstick by which to estimate it's duration. That meant he realized he would spend more money than planned on the world's first photo-documentation of war – but he didn't have the foggiest idea of what his total outlay might be. It would prove financially ruinous.

Though historically significant, photographs of regions where fierce battles once raged are typically low in human interest. Artists as well as photographers wrestled with this dilemma and never found a satisfactory solution. Unusual terrain gave men behind cameras something with which to work. At Gettysburg, immense boulders that were left behind when glaciers melted provide an awesome spectacle nearly two centuries after they became silent witnesses to the biggest battle fought on the continent of North America. Brady and his operatives didn't arrive at the once-peaceful Pennsylvania village until the contending armies had left. It would have made no difference if they had been there on July 1, 1863. They couldn't have captured on glass any of the dramatic movements that took place during three days of ceaseless combat.

Fortunately for us, members of the Brady Studio shot good pre- and post-battle photographs of numerous key figures who took part in combat at Gettysburg.

Hundreds of photos credited to the Brady Studio were made by persons unknown or by operatives who were in the process of leaving Brady. This one made in front of Petersburg, Virginia, is beyond dispute the work of Brady. Wearing his distinctive field outfit, Brady stands to the right of center in the photo. As this shot was being made, Rebel shells began screaming toward the spot.

LEFT: *Visiting the Antietam battleground shortly after the bloodiest single day in American history, Abraham Lincoln may have turned down use of the chair provided by the photographer because he was proud of his towering six-foot-four frame. Clearly, he looked down upon George B. McClellan, commander of the Army of the Potomac (facing him in the photograph), and the bevy of brigadiers who made up most of this group.*

RIGHT: *All of this destruction on the Fredericksburg, Virginia, battlefield resulted from a single projectile. Gunners of the 2nd Massachusetts Heavy Artillery fired numerous 32-pound shells. One of them killed at least three horses.*

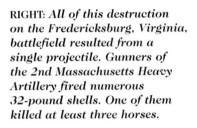

RIGHT: *Boulders that formed Devil's Den gave protection to Rebel sharpshooters at Gettysburg for many hours. One man who didn't make it, however, was found lying near his rifle-musket by photographer Alexander Gardner – who left Brady about the time this powerful image on a glass negative was being printed.*

ABOVE: *John Burns of Gettysburg, whose cottage was on the battlefield. Shown here – after the battle – with his wife, hunting rifle, and crutch, Burns was the most notable civilian hero of the battle. Past 70 years of age, he hobbled into the fight, was wounded three times, and is believed to have taken out one or more Confederates less than half his age.*

RIGHT: *Two weeks after the Battle of Gettysburg, a local describes to Brady how General John F. Reynolds had fallen in or near the woods on the right, below McPherson's Ridge in the background. The general had been hit in the head by a chance Rebel bullet on the first day, July 1, 1863, while trying to mount a holding action against the advancing Confederate forces. Brady may have been aware that Reynolds was practically fighting on home ground, the general having been a native of Lancaster, a town just forty miles to the east of this scene.*

LEFT: *One of many gorges on Lookout Mountain, Tennessee, separated from Missionary Ridge by a valley. Confederate General Braxton Bragg's forces were easily driven off the mountain, but many of them retreated to seemingly impregnable Missionary Ridge. Without orders, a small band of Federals soon charged up the sheer side of the Ridge. Rebels scooted as they came near, and the tide of battle turned as men in blue occupied the Ridge.*

BELOW: *Much of Tennessee, especially along and near its rivers, was battleground. Once Federal troops held the capital of the state, Confederate sharpshooters took to high spots on all major rivers in order to harass the enemy with near impunity. A gunboat in this gorge of the Tennessee River might carry a piece of considerable size – but it couldn't be elevated enough to give any trouble to Rebels perched high above with hand weapons.*

LEFT: *A photographer's portable dark room sat in the center of this picket post close to Atlanta, Georgia. This photo is included as an example of work by a former operative of Brady and is widely but erroneously credited to the Brady Studio. Well before he started south from Chattanooga with the armies of Sherman, George Barnard had gone independent after an apprenticeship with Brady.*

BELOW: *Men of battery B, 1st Pennsylvania Light Artillery, pushed very close to the edge of the Confederate defenses on the Petersburg battleground. The photographer especially wanted to get a good photo of the 12-pound smoothbore Napoleon guns. By the time his camera was ready for use, Rebel gunners had found the range and were dropping shells on this segment of the battleground when the photo was made.*

ABOVE: *A few of many men of C.S. General Richard S. Ewell's command who swarmed confidently upon the Spotsylvania battleground and stayed there when opposing forces pulled out in May, 1864. Logic suggests that they didn't fall in the orderly pattern shown but, like the dead of Antietam, were arranged to the satisfaction of the photographer (who, because of the date, is believed to have been Gardner) before his shutter clicked.*

LEFT: *Some analysts consider this to be a camp scene. However, although the Federal officers and men give the appearance of being thoroughly relaxed, the photo was made behind a protective earthwork. Confederate gunners close to Petersburg, Virginia, knew that the enemy was near – and that if they did not already have the range, they would find it very soon. The photograph was taken in 1865; most of the men shown would have survived to witness the Federal victory at Petersburg, precipitating the fall of Richmond, capital of the Confederacy.*

LEFT: *Captured Richmond, where expected do-or-die resistance by Confederates did not materialize, as seen from an island in the middle of the James River. This little spot, locally called Belle Isle, was considered by its captors to be terribly misnamed. Rebels erected here an open-air stockade in which they confined captured enlisted men in blue under conditions almost as bad as those at Andersonville.*

RIGHT: *Kennesaw Mountain, where the death of Bishop/ General Leonidas Polk was a major incident. Barnard shot this photo to document the thoroughness with which Union troops threw up defensive works as soon as they came close to those of the enemy. Though called "entrenchments" by those who made and used them, these works are above ground. By felling native trees, defenses of this sort could be established very quickly.*

LEFT: *These big siege guns, too heavy for use in the field, were probably produced at the Tredegar Iron Works of Richmond – chief source of Rebel-made guns throughout the war. They were lined up, presumably loaded and ready for action the minute dust columns near the horizon proclaimed that "The Yankees are coming!" Confederates abandoned their capital long before the first contingent of men in blue hove into sight. As a result, this artillery park marks "a battleground that never was."*

THE WEAPONS

"I am sending you all the guns, dear General.
This is a hard fight, and had better all die than lose it."
C.S. General James Longstreet to General Roger Pryor, on the eve of Antietam

Military leaders on both sides went into combat under the assumption
that the war would be fought in Napoleonic style. That is, they expected units of
every size to move as structured military bodies. Highly stylized battlefield performances
that marked very recent European conflicts were planned by many a commander in both
blue and gray. The bayonet had played a crucial and sometimes decisive role in Europe,
so it was expected to do the same thing in the North American conflict. All officers were
told to become adept in the use of the sword, and it was anticipated that the saber
would be a major weapon of cavalry.

All of these preconceptions were demolished when the rifle began to replace the
smoothbore musket. Once rifles began to predominate, most killing took place at relatively
long rather than short range. Pistols and carbines were rarely seen during the first few
armed clashes, but they soon appeared as specialized rapid-fire weapons that were often
the personal property of men who carried them.

In spite of the fact that most officers on both sides soon gave theoretical acceptance
to the fact that this war would be quite different from those of the recent past, many
or most of them clung to the use of Napoleonic tactics and outmoded hand weapons.
Washington was especially reluctant to make rapid-fire weapons standard issue; quarter-
masters feared that use of them would lead to extravagant waste of ammunition.
Horse-drawn field artillery plus big guns were manufactured wholesale in the North
and largely captured or imported in the South. Despite their power, such pieces
accounted for only a fraction of the deaths in combat.

Use of the term "battery" was loose and inconsistent. It was often employed to
designate a single gun. The photo shows a fortification that held at least nine heavy pieces, yet it
was also known simply as a battery. Lethal as they were, big guns accounted for only a
small fraction of casualties incurred in combat. Projectiles were seldom absolutely uniform
in size, tens of thousands of fuses had to be cut by hand, and targets were not often known
with pinpoint accuracy. This powerful battery spewed an average of at least 1,000 pounds
of iron for each enemy soldier it took out.

LEFT: *At an unidentified landing on the James River, the transport* Silver Star *is ready to take on dozens of caissons. Each was built to carry about 150 rounds for horse-drawn field artillery. When attached to a limber, a four-wheel artillery vehicle was formed. Though numerous individual Federal batteries ran low on ammunition during prolonged battles, there was never a widespread shortage of caissons or ammunition available to Union gunners.*

LEFT: *Only a small segment of the supply depot at City Point, Virginia, is shown here. Enough big guns, mortars, and cannon balls are visible to indicate at a glance that from the beginning of the war the vast industrial superiority of the North was a significant factor in the ultimate outcome.*

RIGHT: *Thousands of cannon balls, neatly stacked, were stockpiled at the Washington Arsenal. Lincoln feared that Confederate raiders would swoop down on the capital, so he saw to it that Washington was never short of ammunition and was ringed by forts that made it one of the most strongly fortified cities in the world. In addition, Lincoln demanded that commanders station large bodies of troops at the capital, no matter how desperately they were needed elsewhere.*

RIGHT: *Civil War marine mines were called torpedoes, because of their elongated shape. Thousands of them were used by opposing forces, and some of them took out powerful warships. From this torpedo station, explosives such as the one lying between two men in the foreground, were planted in a nearby river with the hope that they would blow an enemy vessel sky high.*

LEFT: *A mortar had a short range, but was capable of throwing its projectiles high enough to go over enemy defenses and, hopefully, into ranks of defenders of an installation. This 13-inch piece, so powerful that it was dubbed "The Dictator," was used by Federal forces in the lengthy siege of Petersburg.*

RIGHT: *Numerous gunboats used on dozens of rivers were especially designed and built to carry mortars. When the enemy occupied a relatively high bluff, naval guns couldn't be elevated enough to be effective. Mortars threw their projectiles so high that they could reach the majority of the positions against which they were used.*

LEFT: *Mobility was the most valued attribute of horse-drawn field artillery. Though it was very light by comparison with huge naval and siege guns, a single piece of this sort could play a crucial role in a battle. If situated so that it could enfilade (hit the flank of) advancing enemies, a light gun could throw havoc into the ranks of attackers.*

RIGHT: *Big guns at an incredibly tidy Fort Totten, near Rock Creek, one of the bastions that ringed Washington, were kept at the ready around the clock. Stacked rifles, at center and right of center in the photo, behind smartly turned out buglers, were at hand for use in case enemy forces should reach the parapet and try to storm it.*

LEFT: *Light artillery units tried to drill several times a day before going into combat. This was a three-gun battery, the Keystone (the third gun not shown), which left Philadelphia for Washington in mid-August, 1862. It was assigned to defense of the capital for more than a year, after which it joined the Army of the Potomac and took part in the pursuit of the Army of Northern Virginia. This battery was one of only a few units that suffered not a single casualty.*

RIGHT: *Daggers in belts, these 4th Michigan Infantry men and their officer gained a fine reputation for their courage and organisation. Instead of their standard muzzleloaders, however, they would have preferred repeaters such as the Spencer, or the Colt revolving rifle. Best of all would have been the Henry rifle, of which, starting in 1863, the Ordnance Department bought 1,731, while state and private purchases accounted for a further 8,372 – small figures compared with the one-and-a-half million muzzleloading rifle muskets bought for Union soldiers during the war. It is tempting to speculate by how much the war could have been shortened if the Union had seized the opportunity of issuing more Henrys to the troops.*

RIGHT: *Every infantryman was issued a bayonet about 15 inches long, which he attached to the muzzle of his musket or rifle. Bayonet drill was standard among all infantry units on both sides. Despite frequent occurrence of such phrases as "Give 'em the cold steel, boys!" the bayonet was seldom used, except when ammunition was exhausted.*

LEFT: *Possibly but not positively, half of the members of a gun crew took artificial positions at the photographer's request. Mounted on wheels, this big piece could be swung around a wide arc. Hence it was far more versatile than a fixed piece of similar size.*

BELOW: *Preparing for the siege of Yorktown, Virginia, Federal forces put three powerful guns in Battery No. 1. Few photographs reveal details of such guns more clearly than this. Shot by Alexander Gardner, this photo was made shortly before he left Brady in order to operate independently.*

LEFT: *Fort Corcoran, Virginia, was yet another installation built for the defense of Washington. Canister shot, an anti-personnel ammunition consisting of steel or lead balls bolted together between plates, is stacked at the lower left. When used at 150 yards or less, canister was far more lethal than traditional cannon balls or fuse-detonated shells. When fired, the round would break apart, scattering the deadly balls in all directions.*

LEFT: *Invented by Union admiral John Dahlgren, the Dahlgren gun had a distinctive bottle shape that allowed very heavy powder charges to be used, which gave the weapon great range and velocity. It was the state of the art in heavy artillery during the Civil War.*

RIGHT: *This big fellow located in Fort Johnston at Charleston, S.C., bears no markings to indicate its range. Since it is pointed toward Fort Sumter – barely visible at center left in the photo – its range had to be at least three miles, otherwise it would have been futile to use it against the Confederate-held installation perched on an artificial island built with granite "leavings" that were shipped from the northeast.*

LEFT: *Men of a battery mounted inside an unidentified fort willingly "froze" for the photographer during a routine drill. As much as these gunners practised set routines, formality frequently and understandably went by the wayside under fire during the heat of battle.*

RIGHT: *A photographer snapped this view of a small segment of the Washington Arsenal. One gun was properly pointed toward the Virginia side of the Potomac River, but its mate was headed in the opposite direction – perhaps at the request of the photographer.*

LEFT: *Some analysts hold that this 200-pound Rodman was the biggest gun to see active service during the war. Its huge projectiles screamed – not toward Fort Sumter or some other military objective – but toward the city of Charleston.*

RIGHT: *A gun of any size was rarely hauled into place before a defensive work had been built to protect it. This piece, believed to have been an eight-incher, sat on a bank of the Tennessee River. Well protected in a remote spot, it may have constituted the entire battery.*

RIGHT: *No matter how well it was protected by sandbags, a big gun could go out of action by bursting due to metal fatigue. Huge chunks of iron near the center of the photo represent what was left when an immense Parrott blew apart on its 36th shot. Widely known as the Swamp Angel, the gun was mounted on Morris Island in a bid to terrorize citizens of Charleston. Its 200-pound projectiles shrieked loudly during the 9,700 yards they traversed before hitting the city, so civilians may have had time to run for cover when they heard the eerie sound.*

WAR ON THE WATER

"The biggest guns of our warships have fired until they became too hot for use, but Charleston refuses to surrender."

U.S. Admiral Samuel F. DuPont, submitting his resignation after having unleashed everything he had upon the city

The Federal blockade and the war on water were central to the North's demand for unconditional surrender. Yet the war on land has always received much more attention. Perhaps this is because there were no epic naval struggles involving hundreds of thousands of men and countless casualties.

Yet in at least two instances the war on the water was high drama with far-reaching impact. The drawn battle between the C.S.S. *Virginia* (formerly U.S.S. *Merrimack*) and the U.S.S. *Monitor* is universally described as having "changed naval warfare forever." The victory of the U.S.S. *Kearsage* over the commerce raider C.S.S. *Alabama* spelled the beginning of the end for the Confederacy as clearly as did Gettysburg.

Numerous aspects of the naval war on water were significant but are often overlooked. Ponderous warships capable of belching immense quantities of iron have received much more attention than the modest gunboats that operated on rivers. Yet these smaller craft were central to victories on land at Fort Donelson and many other points.

What's more, they played a vital role in cutting the Confederacy in two.

In 1861 the U.S. Navy was made up of nearly obsolete vessels so scattered that few of them could take part in the blockade. Vast access to money and industrial power soon enabled U.S. Secretary of the Navy Gideon Welles to preside over one of the most formidable navies in the world. C.S. Secretary of the Navy Stephen Mallory started with nothing and was perpetually short of funds and industrial resources. Hence he was forced to take innovative steps.

Brady and his operatives did a superb job of capturing some of the high drama and colorful events that marked this epic struggle on rivers and seas.

Gunboats such as this one, designed for use on rivers, were lightly armed by comparison with sea-going warships. Yet the 100-pound Parrott it carried on its gun deck was bigger and more powerful than the majority of guns mounted in fortresses, as is perhaps being explained to the civilian believed to be Brady (left, in straw hat) and one of his assistants.

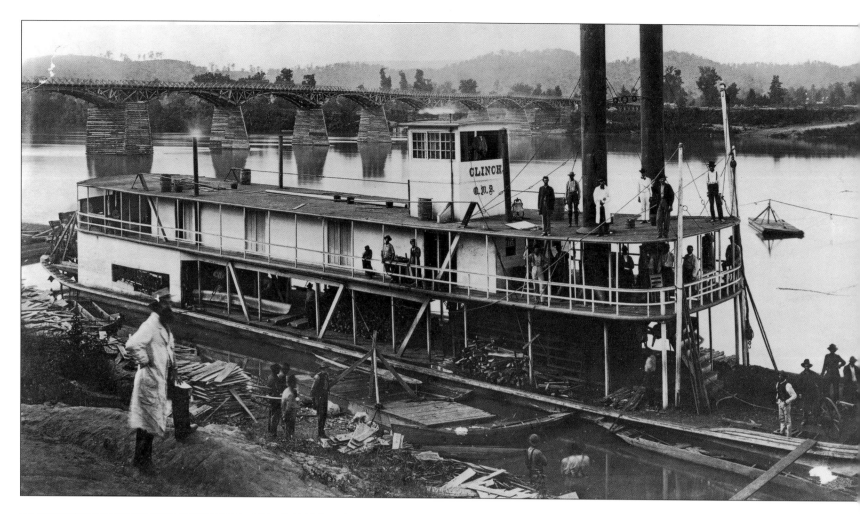

LEFT: *The wood-burning river steamer* Clinch *operated chiefly on the Tennessee River. A glance at this and* Chickamauga *(shown below right) reveals that the two vessels were quite different in design. The fellow standing at the lower left in this photo has long been believed to be Mathew Brady. As was often the case, all loading/unloading was halted while the picture was taken.*

BELOW LEFT: *Lacking capacity to produce great numbers of huge warships, Confederates decided to "think small." From the Biblical story of David and Goliath, the name of the brash challenger of the giant was applied to a needle-shaped vessel operated by a crew of four. This shallow-submerging submarine mounted a torpedo on a spur protruding from its bow. The torpedo was filled with up to 100 pounds of powder. Though no tiny David played a decisive role in battle, Gideon Welles offered a reward of $30,000 for the destruction or capture of any of these early submarines.*

BELOW: *The side-wheel Union transport* Chickamauga *also operated chiefly on the Tennessee River. When tied up to take on or unload huge quantities of supplies, members of the crew of the steamer washed clothing and hung it on lines to dry.*

LEFT: *Virginia's little Pamunkey River was often crowded bank-to-bank with ships. The Ohio-based U.S.S.* New Jersey, *at the right in the photo, towers above a cluster of barges and the paddle-steamer* Wenonah. *White House manor, part of the property in which Mrs. Robert E. Lee had a lifetime interest, was also located on this stream.*

LEFT: *Following Federal reverses at Spotsylvania, Virginia, Grant ordered the evacuation of this once-important supply base adjacent to Port Royal on the Rappahannock River. To facilitate movement of huge quantities of supplies from shore to waiting transports, a pontoon bridge strong enough to bear up under heavy loads was hastily erected.*

RIGHT: *The number of vessels in this fleet, photographed on a major river, helps to underscore the vital role that inland waterways played in the transportation of men, guns, and supplies. Control of even a few miles of an important river put the enemy at a disadvantage.*

RIGHT: *Any time a river did not flow smoothly, gunboats and transports faced trouble. Huge ropes stashed on shore suggest that they were needed when a vessel wanted to pass these rapids on the Tennessee River.*

LEFT: *Commanders didn't willingly send armies to points that could not be reached by river. Total cargo carried by steamers such as the* Wauhatchie, *the* Missionary, *and a multitude of others greatly exceeded total tonnage moved by rail. That meant control of the rivers was vital. Here, the two vessels identified lie close to the base of a spur of Lookout Mountain – a Confederate bastion that crumbled because attackers had no shortage of vital supplies.*

RIGHT: *A sizeable crew of men from the Quartermaster's Corps was assigned to build a river steamer from scratch. Some of the artisans who worked on this vessel had extensive experience as civilian ship builders prior to the onset of hostilities.*

LEFT: *A vital but often overlooked aspect of the naval struggle centered in the collection of duties on imported goods. In his First Inaugural, Lincoln promised to keep this up – knowing that this was the biggest prewar source of revenue for the Federal government. Temporarily moored at Alexandria, Virginia, this revenue cutter patrolled coastal waters to police smugglers.*

LEFT: *The gunboat* Miami *spent months on patrol duty on the James River. These officers are just back from a riverside hunt or are about to launch one. Inability of the dog at the left in the photo to keep still for a few seconds helps to underscore understanding of why Brady and his operatives photographed so few animals.*

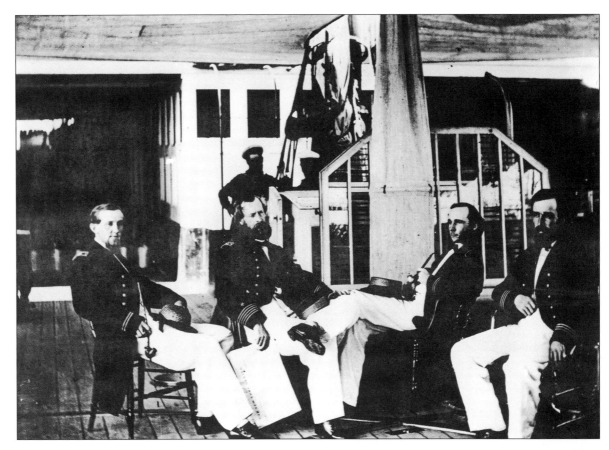

RIGHT: *Compared with life on immense warships, life on river boats was relaxed. In addition, each officer had several times the number of "between decks" square feet than could be expected on a warship. Some experts who have examined this photo believe that the officer at the extreme right in the photo is U.S. Naval Academy graduate and future admiral George Dewey.*

RIGHT: *Officers used the abundant between-decks space of gunboats for recreation and letter-writing, as well as loafing.*

LEFT: *Like their comrades ashore, crew members of warships such as the Passiac usually turned out in mass for occasional "divine services."*

LEFT: *Every Federal ironclad built in the general style of the U.S.S. Monitor was called a monitor. Officers who gathered on the deck of the Mahopac provide a perspective on the size of the revolving gun turret that was a distinctive feature of every monitor.*

RIGHT: *Able-bodied seamen had none of the luxuries enjoyed by officers. Size of the crew of the gunboat Hunchback is proof positive that these fellows were crowded close together when they slept. The banjo-strumming contraband and the newspaper reader close to the left may have been showing off. It's equally possible, however, that they were carefully guided as to their pose by the photographer.*

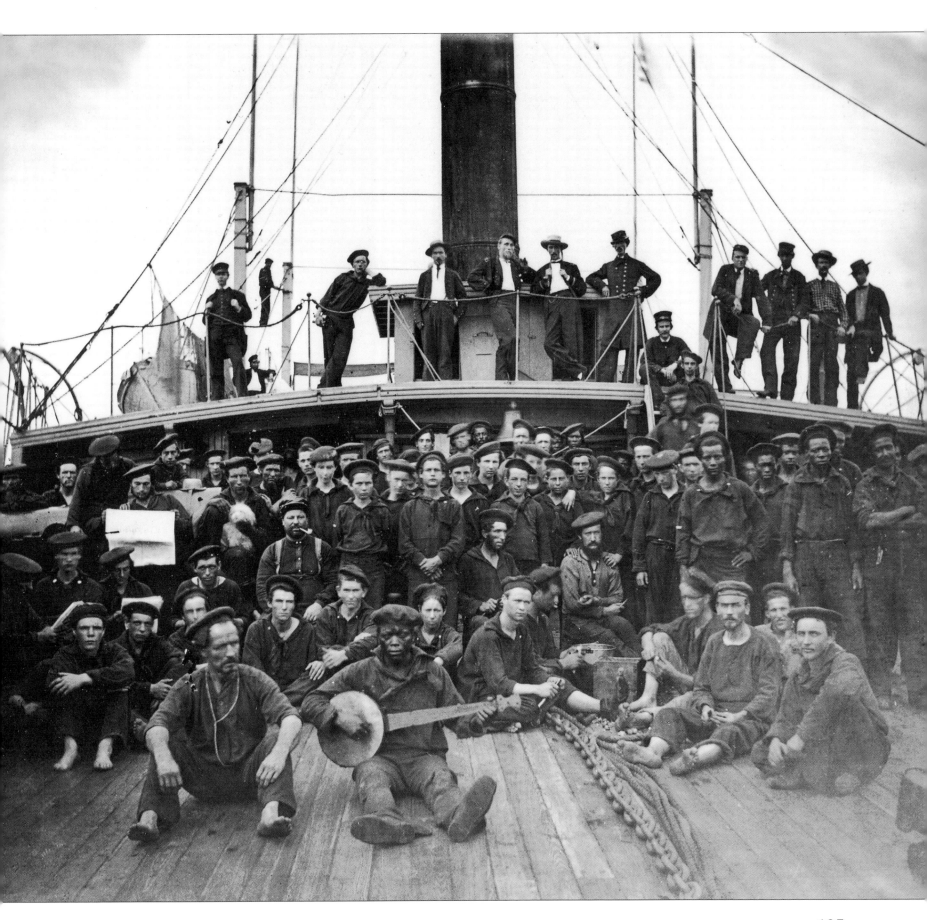

LEFT: *Some gunboats carried only a bowchaser, one piece at the bow; others, such as the* Mendota, *had several pieces much heavier than field artillery used on land.*

RIGHT: *A few monitors such as the* Onandaga, *photographed off a landing on the James River, had two turrets. Construction of this type required a very long vessel, and experience showed that attempts to "double the fire power of a monitor" made the ship slow and clumsy.*

RIGHT: *Leaders on both sides converted numerous unarmed vessels into gunboats. Once a ferry, this unidentified craft carries a single bow gun considerably heavier than most of the types arming these river boats.*

LEFT: *The side-wheel gunboat* Commodore Barney *was equipped with only one smokestack – but proudly flew three flags that flapped in the wind when the camera snapped.*

LEFT: *Members of the crews of warships sometimes had no opportunity to put their feet on solid ground for weeks or months at a time. Here, crew members of an unidentified river boat swarmed ashore at a point where a photographer was waiting. Men who served on small gunboats were usually able to go ashore at frequent intervals.*

RIGHT: *This powder monkey looks to be about nine or ten years old. Able-bodied seamen were too big effectively to feed big naval guns with powder lugged from cramped magazines. Hundreds of small boys were recruited for naval duty and they played an overlooked but vital role in the war on the rivers and high seas.*

TRANSPORTATION

"Order your wagonniers to use the whip; every moment lost is worth the lives of a thousand men."

C.S. General Nathan Bedford Forrest to General Braxton Bragg, who was moving toward Chickamauga, Tennessee – slowly

Where usable roads existed, they were heavily used. Most traffic was made up of columns of marching soldiers sometimes miles in length, plus wagon trains whose tails weren't visible from their heads. Relatively good roads fostered transportation of wounded men to field and permanent hospitals by ambulance.

Railroads, in which the North held an initial significant advantage that was never reduced, were vital. Lincoln's first suspension of the time-honored writ of *habeas corpus* was made because railroad links between the capital and the North were considered to be in serious jeopardy.

Where bridges had been destroyed and no fords were available, rivers constituted major barriers to the movement of troops, guns, and supplies. This led to dramatic progress in the design and use of pontoons, which were always more abundant among Federal forces than among their enemies.

Rivers and canals were all-important in the constant struggle to get men and goods where they were needed. In addition to the fact that transports abounded on these waterways – even on many small ones – they were often dotted with gunboats. Many of these played significant roles in major clashes, such as those at Vicksburg, where Grant eventually succeeded in getting his men south of the Rebel citadel on the east side of the Mississippi River.

Horses and mules were basic to land transportation. Thousands of animals had officers on their backs, and multitudes of them pulled wagons, guns, supplies, and ambulances. They did not have a major role in the Brady Studio photographs because horses seldom remained still while a collodion-covered glass plate was being exposed.

Huge locomotive smokestacks, typically topped by spark arresters, made splendid targets for the enemy. A civilian, who is not dressed in typical Brady fashion but does resemble the photographer, is perched casually on the war-damaged locomotive.

LEFT: *An unidentified company of McClellan's infantry waits to board a train for Alexandria, Virginia. Judging by its appearance, engine No. 156 has very recently become a part of the U.S. Military Railroad system.*

LEFT: *Though coal was the preferred fuel for locomotives, a great many of them had to "make do" with wood – of which there was an abundant supply. With the camera focused on activity in a depot of the U.S. Military Railroad, a slight movement by the colonel just left of center in the photo caused his faced to be blurred.*

RIGHT: *Engineers on both sides did their best to fortify railroad bridges. Confederates did such a good job at the Chattahoochee River that Sherman decided a direct attack would be futile. He had a pontoon bridge thrown across the river about eight miles north of the bridge, near Soap Creek, and managed to avoid a deadly direct confrontation.*

RIGHT: *When Federal forces beat a hasty retreat after Second Bull Run, every depot and rail center in the region was filled with abandoned equipment and debris. Here, a clean-up has started at a small yard on the Orange and Alexandria Railroad.*

LEFT: *This sturdy pontoon across the James River at Deep Bottom, Virginia, is almost but not quite ready for use. When guns and horses crossed such a structure, every effort was made to cover its surface with a thick layer of hay. Men did not march across a pontoon; they were ordered to straggle – to break step. Many feet hitting a bridge like this in cadence could have caused it to snap.*

LEFT: *Long before the war ended, Federal engineers devised a light and portable canvas "pontoon boat." When a quantity of these had been pulled by wagon to a point of use, even a wide river became no obstacle in less than an hour. This pontoon boat was photographed at Rappahannock Station, Virginia, in March 1864.*

RIGHT: *Almost every river of any size was crossed by one or more pontoons before the war ended. Seen on a map, Virginia's James River appears to have been inconsequential in size – but close to its mouth it was more than a mile wide. Located at an undesignated point on the James, this lengthy pontoon saw heavy traffic – but blocked the passage of transports and gunboats.*

B-301

LEFT: *In many instances, officers directed cavalry units to go along river banks instead of crossing them. When no hay was available, a pontoon was rarely strong enough to stand up under the pounding of the feet of 1,000-pound war horses.*

RIGHT: *Unionist civilians who lived within a short distance of a Federal pontoon and who had passes were often permitted to use this all-important transportation device. It was not unusual for a bevy of civilians to arrive in a vehicle driven by a contraband.*

RIGHT: *Baggage of soldiers traveled by wagon. A commander intent on winning battles imposed strict limits on the number of baggage wagons that could go along with his men. This one transported the entire headquarters baggage of U. S. Grant.*

RIGHT: *"Corduroy roads" were not surfaced with ribbed fabric of this name, but were built with sections of the trunks of small native trees. A wagon driver's teeth often jolted when his vehicle was on a stretch of corduroy. He didn't complain; without the improvised hard surface he might have mired down to the tops of his large rear wheels.*

LEFT: *Canals such as the Baltimore & Ohio played a major role in transportation. U.S. General Benjamin F. Butler ordered the construction of Dutch Gap Canal on the James River for military purposes and used it accordingly. It continued to be a significant transportation artery for many years after the conflict ended.*

BELOW: *U. S. Grant, seeking a way to get south of Vicksburg on the east side of the Mississippi River, used most of the manpower of his army to build canals. This one on the James River was cut by a relatively small number of men in a short time.*

RIGHT: *To General Butler – a prewar attorney, not an engineer – it appeared that a heavily guarded big bend in the James River was a major impediment in his planned move on Richmond. When finished, Dutch Gap Canal was big enough to float a transport and a monitor at the same time. It did bypass those powerful Confederate batteries – but failed to enable Butler's command to reach the Rebel capital.*

RIGHT: *At many points, the James River buzzed with activity. Though most of them are too far away to be seen clearly, a single photo caught at least a dozen transports and gunboats plus the monitor Casco (nearest of the vessels, without its turret) in languid movement.*

LEFT: *A photographer who found men engaged in an ambulance drill probably asked them to pose at spots of his choice. Though similar to the two-wheel avalanche, the ambulance was more stable. Tens of thousands of them were built for transportation of wounded men. Because ambulances were especially comfortable and light, hundreds were commandeered by officers for their personal use or for transportation of their wives and children.*

RIGHT: *When a road had borne heavy wagon traffic for decades, wheels of vehicles often cut so deeply into its surface that it became locally known as "the sunken road." Because such topography offered splendid cover, a sunken road was seen as a godsend by troops who occupied it. The Sunken Road on the Antietam battlefield became one of the notable landmarks of the bloodiest day in American history.*

LEFT: *The U. S. Sanitary Commission, established to give soldiers supplies and aid not available through military channels, became an immense organization before war's end. Its members typically used four-horse wagons whose rear wheels were noticeably larger than those in the front. Men lined up to the right of the center in the photo are Sanitary Commission workers. The man on horseback, obviously in charge, was too far from the camera for him to be identified as an officer or a civilian leader.*

RIGHT: *Though it was tiny by comparison with better-known rivers, the Pamunkey played a significant role in transportation for many months. A supply depot built at White House Landing (once the home of Mrs. Robert E. Lee) has so many barges crowded close to one another that it is impossible to count them accurately.*

FEATS OF ENGINEERING

"The art of bridge building advanced more during 1861-1865 than during the previous one thousand years."

U.S. General George G. Meade

Railroads and their bridges were so vital that numerous regiments detailed to guard them never saw combat. The building of fortifications was highly specialized work, ranking so high in importance that only a small percentage of West Point graduates who were at the top of their class were assigned to the Corps of Engineers, U. S. Army. As a member of that corps, Robert E. Lee worked for a time at Fort Pulaski, Georgia, and is credited with having helped to make the fortification seized by the state to be very difficult to re-capture.

Because they were rarely involved in combat, even top engineers seldom saw their names in headlines. They went about their work quietly and unobtrusively, but accomplished some truly amazing feats, some of which were completed before the outbreak of war. Bridges at Washington experienced war-time traffic at least ten times the maxim expected when they were built. Yet at war's end, these bridges remained sturdy and dependable. Unfinished Fort Sumter at Charleston was so strong in 1861 that Confederate bombardment from shore barely dented its walls. Later, the fortress withstood an incredibly heavy cannonade from big naval guns.

Herman Haupt, an 1835 graduate of the U.S. Military Academy, was the outstanding engineer of the war. With the rank of colonel, he was put in charge of the vast U.S. Military Railroad System. Immediately after having become a brigadier in September 1862, he resigned his commission and served thereafter without rank or pay. He developed and built a portable truss that bore his name and that was widely used in bridge building.

Abraham Lincoln was astonished when he saw the bridge that engineers had built over Potomac Creek during the spring of 1862. "That man, Haupt," he told cabinet members, "has built a bridge 400 feet long and nearly 100 feet high, over which loaded trains run every hour. Upon my word, there is nothing in it but bean-poles and corn stalks." Part of the first military railroad built during the war, it enabled Aquia Creek to be linked with Fredericksburg.

150

LEFT: *Once a Confederate town or city fell, Federal engineers swarmed into it and started rebuilding its infrastructure – usually badly damaged during its reduction. Here the conquered town is Fredericksburg, Virginia, where rail track near the Potomac River is being repaired.*

LEFT: *Once Forts Henry and Donelson fell to U. S. Grant, rivers took Federal forces into the heart of Tennessee. The state capitol, located on the top of a hill in Nashville, is barely visible at the left of center in this photo. This segment of a lengthy railroad trestle was built under the supervision of army engineers. When they had finished their work in a conquered town or city, the army had a sturdy permanent base from which to move forward.*

LEFT: *Photographers rarely managed to get members of an engineers' unit together long enough to make a photograph. These fellows, who may have been relaxing between assignments, belonged to the 8th New York State Militia. Their black servant was placed, as usual, where he would show up at the extreme left in the photo. Like many other Northern militia units, the 8th New York wore gray uniforms.*

BELOW: *Confederate rail centers such as Chattanooga near Atlanta had yards with multiple sets of tracks plus fully equipped roundhouses (upper left) for locomotive maintenance. A large body of evidence indicates that, prior to his advance into Georgia, Grant instructed Sherman simply to crush Rebel forces that opposed him. In his letters and dispatches, Atlanta emerged as a major target only about the time Sherman reached the Chattahoochee River.*

RIGHT: *Engineers threw up bridges such as this one on the Orange and Alexandria Railroad during a few days' work. They then moved on to another job, knowing that a permanent camp of guards would be established to try to keep their handiwork intact. Brady or one of his operatives probably had a camera ready for use when a civilian in a stovepipe hat wandered into the foreground and was caught too near the camera that was focused upon the newly constructed bridge and the front end of a railroad train.*

LEFT: *Engineers who constructed the massive earthworks of Battery Rodgers had been told to make them sturdy, since they were a part of the defensive network that ringed Washington. The open doors of these bombproofs suggest that the garrison stationed here had decided that a strong Confederate attack upon the capital was not likely to take place, despite Abraham Lincoln's constant agonizing over such a possibility.*

RIGHT: *Washington's Chain Bridge was built before the war by men of the U.S. Army's Corps of Engineers. During four years of constant heavy traffic, it rarely suffered damage sufficient to warrant a repair job.*

RIGHT: *A long bridge across the Cumberland River at Chattanooga was even more flimsy than the one an astonished Lincoln said had been built of bean-poles and cornstalks. Work by a Confederate demolition crew made it unusable until Federal engineers completed a hasty repair job.*

LEFT: *Anticipating large movements of troops, engineers built a new bridge across the Tennessee River at Chattanooga. Despite heavy reliance upon native timber rather than stone, this structure remained functional throughout the period when big battles were being fought nearby.*

LEFT: *Engineers erected a long and tall trestle bridge in a remote region near Whiteside, Virginia. Their structure was vital to the operation of the Nashville and Chattanooga Railroad, over which a constant stream of traffic flowed.*

RIGHT: *Men of the U.S. Army Corps of Engineers designed and built Washington's Long Bridge across the Potomac River before war started. This was the chief bridge used by Federal forces on the fateful morning when the invasion of Virginia was launched. Troops who had crossed the Long Bridge met no resistance when they reached Arlington, but Colonel Elmer Ellsworth (a Lincoln favorite) was shot and killed by the owner of a small hotel there.*

LEFT: *Engineers usually built pontoon bridges in response to a military emergency. Once completed, however, a structure might remain in place for months or even years. It was not likely to cease to be used unless it was destroyed by the enemy or its construction materials were critically needed elsewhere.*

LEFT: *Among general officers, George G. Meade probably had the most respect for engineers. Photographed here as a brigadier before being named commander of the Army of the Potomac, Meade rarely made a move without consulting his engineers. Numerous other commanders acted first and consulted later – often with disastrous results.*

RIGHT: *The U.S. Army Corps of Engineers built numerous sturdy aqueducts during the quarter-century before the outbreak of war. One such ran above the Cabin John Bridge about seven miles from Washington. Built around 1860 under the direction of Montgomery C. Meigs, the bridge itself was 105 feet high and and 20 feet wide above the arch, and was topped by an aqueduct designed to be inconspicuous. Resting on top, it appears simply to be part of the bridge.*

RIGHT: *Engineers responsible for this unfinished bridge used novel techniques developed by Herman Haupt. Prefabricated segments that he designed for quick assembly on the spot permanently altered the work of bridge-building in loyal and in seceded states.*

LEFT: *Brady and his operatives had very few opportunities to make photos showing the work of Confederate engineers. Accompanying Federal forces to Bull Run, they were struck by the elaborate defenses that had been thrown up by Rebels at Centreville, Virginia. Seen from a distance of half-a-mile or so, this seemingly formidable work dotted with big guns appears to be a major obstacle. Actually flimsy, it held nothing but "Quaker guns," logs cut to look like cannon. Two are clearly visible in the photograph.*

RIGHT: *In the vicinity of Manassas Junction, Virginia, desperate Confederate engineers used just about anything they could get to erect fortifications. Not having the time or the materials with which to fashion fascines and gabions, they resorted to empty barrels as substitutes at one point on the Bull Run battlefield. Alexander Gardner, who made this photo, was then a full-time employee of Brady; according to customs of the time, his work was credited to the Brady Studio.*

LEFT: *Earth-packed wicker gabions, which Confederates desperately needed but often did not have, stand at the left center of this photo. It was taken inside an undesignated but once-formidable Confederate fortification that had been reduced to rubble by Federal gunners. Heavy guns have been removed or lie in fragments among the rubble.*

RIGHT: *During the long siege of Petersburg, Virginia, dozens of fortifications were erected. Some were almost as sturdy as permanent installations, despite the fact that they were open-air earthworks. Members of the garrison of this beautifully engineered work defended it from gabion-lined trenches.*

LEFT: *Engineers designed Fort Stevens as part of the chain of installations that made Washington one of the most heavily fortified cities in the world. An immense earthwork, cut only by a sally port, served to protect its battery of heavy guns. Engineers probably advised members of the garrison to throw up chevaux-de-frise (formally constructed wooden obstacles) in front of the earthworks, but scarcity of materials or pure laziness led a commander to settle for a flimsy row of branches from trees.*

BELOW: *Fort Sumter at Charleston, South Carolina, was subjected to merciless pounding by big guns over a period of many months. Never finished and never garrisoned before Maj. Robert Anderson moved his men from nearly Fort Moultrie without authorisation from Washington at the start of the war, its ponderous walls were barely pockmarked when the Federal blockade of Charleston was launched. Eventually pounded to the ground, it was not rebuilt. Today's visitors go to the artificial island on which Sumter was built expecting to get a good look at its ruins. Many are disappointed to find a nearly barren area that holds few visible reminders that a mighty five-sided installation once stood here and was the first target of Confederate guns.*

SPECIALISTS

"The mobile telegraph is the artery through which the blood of the Army of the Potomac flows."

U.S. General Ulysses S. Grant

Large numbers of soldiers had training or experience that made them more valuable in some other role than that of infantryman. Some of these men were temporarily or permanently assigned to work as telegraphers. Others were hastily trained so that they would be useful in the brand-new Signal Corps.

Numerous volunteers entered the military in order to serve in a special capacity. Many regiments had their own bands, made up of experienced musicians. A great many drummers were boys, the majority of whom were under the age of 18 when they managed to enlist. These young fellow, along with other specialists in uniform, were subject to the same regulations as those that governed the conduct of soldiers. Largely because a number of drummers deserted, were captured, and punished, Congress enacted and Lincoln signed legislation that forbade the execution of anyone under age 18 years.

Civilians who filled special roles abounded in or near most camps. Substantial numbers of men working full time in what we today would call the media tried to follow every army into the field. These newspaper correspondents and artists were on the payrolls of their employers and were not subject to regulations that applied to soldiers.

Perhaps the most unusual of all specialists were men who called themselves balloonists or aerialists. Confederates lacked experienced men and equipment with which to develop a Balloon Corps, but Federals had the services of Thaddeus Sobieski Constantine Lowe and his experienced assistants. Despite the fact that some commanders were openly contemptuous of these men, they conducted numerous aerial experiments with significant military applications.

Far the best-known balloon of the Civil War was Lowe's Intrepid, *in which he made ascents over several battlefields. From the* Intrepid, *here shown in process of being inflated prior to the Battle of Fair Oaks, Lowe sent the world's first telegram from air to ground. Later, he became the first aerial observer to spot enemy batteries and direct fire against them. He and members of his crew made at least 3,000 ascensions before General Joseph Hooker took steps that caused the Balloon Corps to be disbanded in the spring of 1863.*

LEFT: *A majority of telegraphers were civilians with extensive experience. The clothing – especially hats – of these 11 men sets them apart from comrades in uniform whom they served. Since the telegraph had been developed only a generation earlier, the Civil War was the first conflict in which it was used extensively.*

LEFT: *Illuminating gas extracted from coal competed with hot air as the lifting agent used in early balloons. Confederates, whose experiments with balloons were very limited, had to take their craft to Richmond in order to fill them with coal gas. "Professor" Lowe discovered that the lifting power of hydrogen greatly exceeded that of hot air and coal gas, so he turned to it early in the war. He developed a process by which hydrogen could be produced from sulfuric acid acting on iron filings and mounted his apparatus on the frame of an Army wagon so that he could fill his craft in the field. His* Intrepid *required 32,000 cubic feet of gas. This quantity of hydrogen weighed slightly over 160 pounds, making the Intrepid's lifting power just under 2,300 pounds.*

LEFT: *A few of the telegraphers attached to the Army of the Potomac photographed in July 1863. Grant recognised the importance of the telegraph very early and made more extensive use of it than any other commander on either side. The black civilian at the extreme left in the photo was probably used in stringing wire, which came in 200-pound reels.*

173

LEFT: *Newspaper correspondents and artists, plus men who sold papers, were omnipresent. Yet publishers rarely visited a camp or fortification. The workmen in this photo are oblivious to the presence of Horace Greeley (standing at the right), publisher of the most influential newspaper of the period, the* New York Herald Tribune. *Perhaps the photographer had instructed them to go about their business.*

RIGHT: *Initially, numerous members of the Signal Corps used the telegraph as well as signal flags. Serious squabbles between two bodies of specialists led to a clear-cut division in November 1863, after which the Signal Corps was limited to the use of wig-wag flags. This necessitated the building of taller and taller signal towers, some of which towered over the one shown.*

LEFT: *Correspondents and artists usually traveled in special wagons whose purpose was clearly indicated. These men worked for Horace Greeley's* New York Herald Tribune.

RIGHT: *In a regimental band, the drummer usually had a role secondary to those of men who used wind instruments. These musicians and some of their comrades were photographed in front of a house on Lookout Mountain, Tennessee, that formerly served as a seminary for females. Note the woman in the window at the upper right.*

LEFT: *Many regiments had bands made up of half a dozen or more trained musicians. These fellows, who regaled members of the U.S. Army's 4th Infantry, wore regulation hats, which suggests that each of them was regularly enrolled in the army.*

RIGHT: *Members of a regimental drum corps. These specialists were all-important to the infantry. Each man was required to master at least 15 general drum rolls plus two dozen sets of rhythms with which they guided men on the march and in combat.*

LEFT: *When forming for a dress parade, members of a company or regiment usually placed musicians to their right. These five drummers appear to be considerably older than the tens of thousands of boys who used these instruments to keep marching men in cadence.*

LEFT: *Christopher ("Kit") Carson won prewar fame as a scout and guide. In 1861 he became colonel of the 1st New Mexico with the avowed purpose of fighting Rebels. Most of his wartime years were spent fighting the Apaches, Navajos, and Comanches, however. In this studio portrait he bears little resemblance to the rough-and-ready scout who had helped future General John C. Frémont explore the Rocky Mountains.*

RIGHT: *Some of the many scouts and guides used by the Army of the Potomac were photographed in October 1862, by Alexander Gardner. Believed still to have been a member of the Brady Studio at that time, he persuaded men in varied attire to look as casual as possible. These hardy fellows usually moved ahead of an army, supplying its commander with information about terrain, position of enemy forces, availability of forage for horses, and similar matters.*

RIGHT: *Men camped close to a major city had the benefit of calling upon the local fire department in emergencies. There is no record of how this equipment became so badly damaged. One of the marvels of the war centers in the fact that no large fire was ever reported from the highly-flammable hydrogen used to inflate Lowe's balloons.*

LEFT: *Guards who rode on top of railroad box cars got little recognition or praise. Their special task was extremely hazardous, however. In addition to dangers associated with wrecks, derailments, and other accidents, these men were "sitting ducks" if they passed through an area infested with Confederate sharpshooters or partisan rangers.*

RIGHT: *Though the color-bearer was a regular soldier, his role was very special. During an advance, it was his duty to keep the regimental or national banner at the forefront so that men could be guided by it. Mortality of color-bearers greatly exceeded that among any other specialist. It was not unusual for three or four of these men to be killed or mortally wounded, one after the other, in half-an-hour.*

LEFT: *Men assigned to guard railroad bridges and similar installations were in less danger than those who rode on top of box cars. Still, they were vulnerable to attack 24 hours a day, every day. So many men were required for this special duty that few volunteered for it; instead, entire companies and regiments were assigned to guard duty that might last for months or even years. These fellows, whose ranks include two young boys, have been ordered to see that Rebels did no damage to a bridge of the Orange & Alexandria Railroad.*

THE SICK AND WOUNDED

"Surgeon, do all you can for these pitiful men;
maybe you can ease their pain a little."
C.S. General Nathan B. Forrest to Surgeon J. B. Cowan

All Civil War medics were known as surgeons, whether or not they ever wielded a scalpel. They did the best they could against tremendous obstacles, but their record is dismal. Considerably more men died of illness than from enemy fire. In some camps, the mortality was greater than upon the battlefield.

Surgeons were greatly hampered by lack of knowledge. Yellow fever was not known to be transmitted by mosquitoes, so was attributed to a variety of factors. A Confederate surgeon even came up with a scheme for biological warfare. Great quantities of clothing worn by victims of the fever were collected and shipped north, so that the malady would become rampant in northern cities. Abraham Lincoln was scheduled to receive a package of deluxe "infected" shirts. In the end, nothing came of the scheme.

Surgeons who worked in field hospitals spent most of their time with amputations – performed with no attempt at sanitization. Piles of severed arms and legs became a common sight at a field hospital, and the distinctive rasp of the bone saw was familiar to all members of ambulance teams. Dysentery raged almost everywhere, and probably claimed as many lives as did big guns. Especially during early months of combat, measles laid so many men low that planned movements against the enemy had to be abandoned.

Knowledge about medicinal substances was on a par with understanding of disease. Administration of highly toxic blue mass – a mixture of mercury and chalk – was commonplace. So was use of opium as a pain-killer. So much of it was administered to so many men by surgeons in uniform that great numbers of veterans were addicted to it. With Confederate medical care even worse than Federal, noted analyst Bell Wiley went on record as believing that for every soldier in gray who died in battle, three died in camp from diarrhea, dysentery, typhoid, smallpox, measles, tuberculosis, malaria, or pneumonia.

Close to every major battlefield, men on both sides selected trees to which some of the mortally wounded were taken to die. This "dying tree" adjacent to Marye's Heights at Fredericksburg, Virginia, was photographed soon after having been chosen. Dozens of men who were mortally wounded at Chancellorsville later lay packed closely together and as near the tree as possible.

LEFT: *After the first few months of conflict, most regiments had their own ambulances. This ambulance drill of the 57th New York was held in anticipation that a major confrontation between opposing forces was in the making.*

RIGHT: *The median age of men on both sides who received their first wounds was 22 years. Yet many a battlefield casualty was a child. William Black, who is identified as "a wounded boy," may have been older than he looks. Judging from his appearance, however, he should have been sitting in a fourth-grade classroom somewhere instead of trudging to a battlefield with a musket or a rifle that weighed one-fifth as much as he did.*

RIGHT: *A handful of U.S. Army hospitals were in sturdy permanent buildings. This one, at the corner of Broad and Cherry Streets in Philadelphia, was one of the nation's finest.*

LEFT: *Washington's old and established military hospitals were overflowing long before massive battles began to be fought. In a hasty effort to deal with a critical shortage of beds, Federal officials authorised the erection of numerous temporary hospitals. One of them near the capital occupied a wooden structure that looked like an elongated shed.*

RIGHT: *Interior, Carver General Hospital, Washington. Sadly, such places were rife with medical ignorance, incompetence, and disease. Of the 360,222 Union soldiers who died in the war, 250,000 succumbed to disease and infection of their wounds. Just over 250 million Confederates perished in the conflict, three-quarters of them from sickness rather than from combat.*

LEFT: *Surgeons and stewards of Washington's Harwood Hospital. Sleeves of surgeons bore no insignia, while those of stewards displayed the "double snake" caduceus. Patterns of buttons on jackets and sleeves of the Medical Corps were unique and bore no relationship to similar insignia worn by officers of other branches of the military. On the wards, the U.S. Army relied exclusively upon male nurses until shortages enabled Clara Barton and Dorothea Dix to initiate the use of females. Barton organised a corps of nurses to exacting standards, beginning careers which led to great strides in health care after the war.*

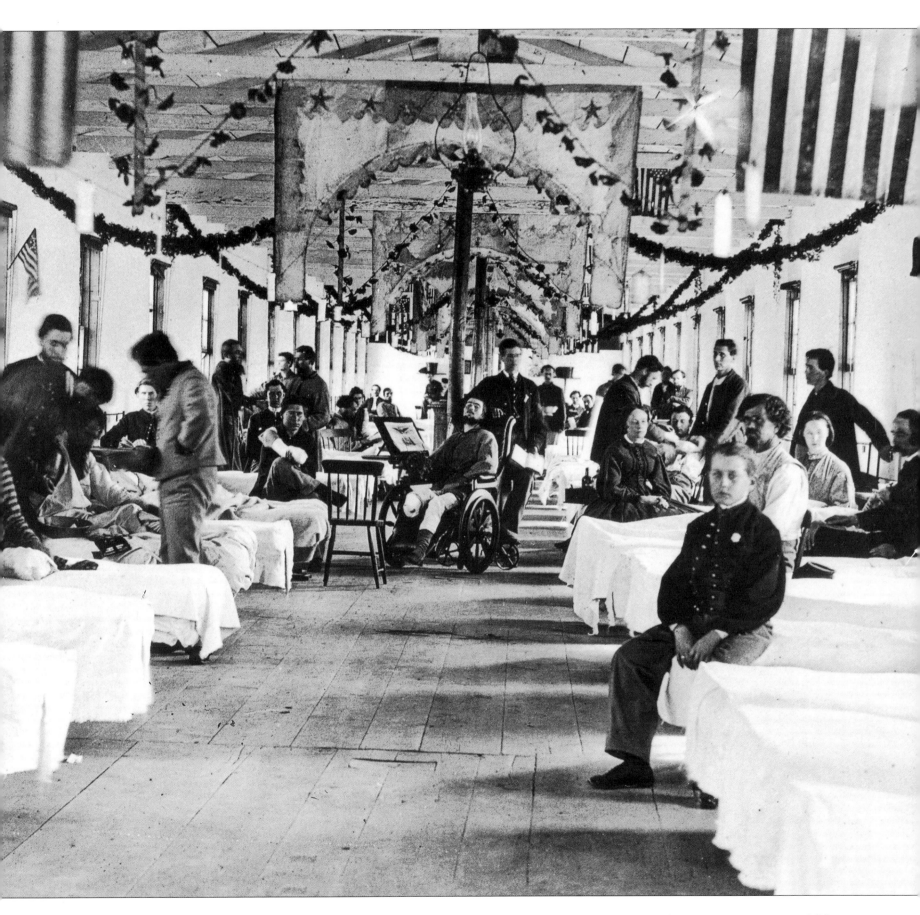

LEFT: *Judging from the cleanliness of the "wounded" soldier, this photograph was probably staged. At a field hospital a genuine casualty would be lucky if he received some anesthesia before surgery, if supplies had not run low. Even if the wounded and sick survived the field hospitals, they faced another ordeal as they were taken to the rear to the hundreds of general hospitals that grew up in the cities of North and South, where gangrene and a range of fatal infections were rife.*

RIGHT: *Confederate hospitals were rarely housed in permanent buildings. This one in Richmond was photographed in April, 1865, after the fall of the city. In the same city, Charleston-born Phoebe Pember overcame male opposition to female nurses and was appointed Chimborazo Hospital's first hospital matron. The hospital she supervised was housed in row after row of wooden buildings and was for a time the largest in the world. It had a capacity of up to 8,000 patients and treated some 76,000 wounded and sick during the war.*

RIGHT: *At Gettysburg, the general hospital consisted of a small "tent city." Even after it was thrown up, many a wounded man was told that there was no room for him there.*

LEFT: *One of numerous hospital tents at Gettysburg devoted exclusively to amputation. The surgeon in the forefront appears ready to take off a mangled leg. General Daniel E. Sickles was probably the best known of Gettysburg's thousands of amputees who survived. He was hit in the right leg. Probably because of his high rank, the mutilated member was removed within half an hour. He donated it to a military museum and reputedly paid a number of visits to it in later life.*

RIGHT: *Surgeons and assistant surgeons of the 164th New York. These men and their comrades were not paid at a rate comparable to earnings of modern physicians. They did enjoy one special benefit, however. A captured surgeon was normally exchanged very quickly.*

LEFT: *Sick and wounded soldiers receiving medication at a tent care center established by the Michigan and Pennsylvania Relief Association. The surgeons of both North and South were grateful for whatever help they could get. In the North there was but one doctor for every 133 men in the ranks, and in the South it was worse – one for every 324.*

LEFT: *The U.S. Sanitary Commission, a civilian agency, collected enormous sums of money with which to buy or build headquarters in many cities. Not subject to military regulations, the Commission's field workers gave medical aid to tens of thousands of wounded and sick men and supplemented a variety of the central government's programs for soldiers. This building in Richmond was not purchased; it was taken over after Confederate military forces fled from the city.*

BELOW: *Large permanent bases, such as Grant's at City Point, Virginia, usually had their own hospitals. These were readily distinguished by the large number of ambulances parked close to them – often having arrived over an "elegant" corduroy road.*

RIGHT: *In the field, workers of the U.S. Sanitary Commission used small buildings or tents as headquarters. Soldiers, who were inordinately grateful for what its mostly female representatives achieved, happily did all they could to make these women comfortable in attractive surroundings. The two women who posed here may have constituted the entire personnel of this outpost.*

RIGHT: *Mary Walker of Oswego, New York, set out to become a physician in an era when few females dared to enter that profession. After graduation from Syracuse Medical College she established a practice in Cincinnati – but failed to get enough clients to make a living. On the outbreak of war she turned to the military and was accepted as a nurse at low but regular pay. Three years later an Ohio regiment agreed to use her as a contract surgeon for six months. She donned the uniform of a male surgeon during this period – but continued to dangle her curls. In the western theater she treated wounded and sick Rebels as well as soldiers in blue. Captured, she spent more than three months in a Confederate prison. Having been awarded a Medal of Honor, she defiantly refused to return it when the award conferred for gallantry was revoked decades later. Dr. Walker wore masculine clothing during the postwar years, and devoted most of her energy to the movement for women's rights.*

THE CARE GIVERS

"Mother Bickerdycke and women like her have done as much to whip the Rebels as has many a well-known regiment."

U.S. General William T. Sherman

Family members and female volunteers did a great deal to boost the morale of fighting men. When a wife managed to pay a visit to her husband in camp, the entire body of men in which he was included was electrified by the presence of a woman among them. In some instances, one or more children came along. They were quickly adopted as company or regimental "pets," and a few of them were formally chosen as mascots. Members of Roman Catholic orders, volunteers working for the U.S. Sanitary Commission, and crusading females plus their followers had virtually the same effect upon a body of homesick men as did a wife.

Even wives who seldom or never visited their husbands in camp were key to morale. Ellen Ewing Sherman, wife of General William T. Sherman, never spent time with her husband while he was encamped, but the couple maintained constant correspondence throughout the war. A volume of *Sherman's Home Letters* sparkles with revelations of the fashion in which Ellen was a care giver at a distance.

Clara Barton, photographed here in 1866 before she founded the American Red Cross, had begun teaching at age 15 and soon started a highly successful free public school. She later went to Washington and became one of the first women who worked for the U.S. Government. In the aftermath of the Baltimore Riot early in the war she gave up her job in the Patent Office in order to become a care giver. She was probably the first person to place newspaper advertisements asking for gifts of supplies badly needed by fighting men. In 1862 the U.S. Surgeon General issued her a pass that enabled her to travel anywhere she wished with ambulances "for the purpose of distributing comforts for the sick and wounded." Late in the war she became the first person actively to seek information about missing men in order to pass it along to relatives. At Andersonville, the infamous Confederate POW camp in Georgia, she identified large numbers of dead and gave members of their families all the information about them that she could. Brady or a member of his staff made this studio portrait of Barton shortly before she gained widespread fame.

LEFT: *A small number of Catholic women who belonged to a variety of orders served full time in military hospitals, most of which were attached to permanent bases. Sister M. M. Joseph of the Sisters of Mercy went to an improvised studio at Hilton Head, South Carolina, to sit for this formal portrait. Her rosary is not only conspicuously visible, it dangles at the precise center of the portrait.*

RIGHT: *White-bearded Brigadier General John J. Abercrombie (seated in the center of the photo) posed with eight members of his staff and the daughter of the U.S. Secretary of the Treasury. The former Kate Chase, now Mrs. Sprague, was among the most noted of Washington beauties. Nothing is known about her ties (if any) with Abercrombie.*

RIGHT: *Garb of Sisters of Charity was quite different from that of Sisters of Mercy. Sister Verona, who also insisted upon holding her rosary so that it could be seen at a glance, was a care giver to men of the Army of the Potomac for a considerable but undated period.*

LEFT: *An occasional female visitor to a camp brought along her own mount, decorously fitted with a side-saddle.*

RIGHT: *Except for Dr. Mary Walker, ladies who visited camps or battlefields usually wore the customary skirt that was so long it dragged across the ground.*

LEFT: *Brady and his operatives often persuaded persons to sit for two or more photos in order to make sure that at least one good one would emerge when they were processed. With Abercrombie and his noted visitor seated squarely in front of a tent, the number of his staff members was reduced by one and they were arranged in quite different order from that for the photograph on the previous page.*

LEFT: *Ladies in this photograph are identified only as "members of the families of officers." Taken at a moment when little wind was blowing, the photo shows the nearly still flag flanked by a boy too young to have been a color-bearer. As is the case with much of the work done by members of the Brady Studio, the flag and boy were probably added for the sake of human interest.*

BELOW: *Females outnumbered males by a ratio of more than 2:1 in this shot made at an unidentified location. This is believed to be a copy made from an original Brady negative. Whoever the photographer was, he added drama by placing a male almost as tall as Abraham Lincoln in the middle of the ladies and dispersing other males at both sides.*

RIGHT: *Colonel James P. McMahon of the 14th New York dutifully pretended for about four seconds to be absorbed in a game of chess. One of the ladies standing behind him was probably his wife, since the small boy at the extreme left in the photo must have been his son. This photograph was made in order to demonstrate to the world that, while encamped, officers and men had time for recreational activities.*

RIGHT: *General George B. McClellan wanted to head an army whose size would greatly exceed that of any force against which he might fight. He was also zealous to have northern industrial production at its peak before engaging in a decisive battle. Abraham Lincoln, his commander-in-chief, craved immediate action. Hence he frequently chided McClellan and described him as being afflicted with "the slows." In this vexatious situation, the commander of the Army of the Potomac regularly turned to his wife – the former Georgiana Heckscher – for solace.*

RIGHT: *Whenever given passes for the purpose, wives and sweethearts plus sisters and offspring flocked to convalescent camps like this one that was located near Alexandria, Virginia. A majority probably had prior knowledge that their loved one was wounded or sick – but alive at least. Those who wore mourning for their visit knew in advance that they had suffered an irreparable loss. An unidentified major general standing close to a post added dignity to this photograph.*

LEFT: *Colorful and daring Major General George Armstrong Custer paid tribute to his wife's care and concern by going with her and his younger brother and aide, Lieutenant Tom Custer, to have a studio portrait made.*

BELOW: *Major General Edward O. C. Ord received a severe wound at Corinth, Mississippi. He recovered sufficiently to take part in the siege of Vicksburg, then led his corps against Jackson, Mississippi. Again severely wounded near Richmond, he recovered enough strength to be present at Appomattox Court House. U.S. Grant, who regarded him highly, reputedly said of Ord that "this man recovered quickly from near-mortal wounds by concentrating his thoughts upon his wife and small daughter."*

RIGHT: *At birth, Thomas Lincoln was nicknamed "Tad" because he reminded his father of a tadpole with a head too large for his body. He was hyperactive and was probably mentally retarded. Still, he gave the war-time president enormous pleasure during hours in which they romped together. Photographed in his favorite outfit – the uniform of a captain – Tad scurried in and out of his father's office many times a day and often played at his feet.*

FLOTSAM AND JETSAM

"There is no such thing as a good prison – in the South or the North."
Congressman Alfred Ely of New York, long a prisoner and a hostage

Little information was recorded concerning soldiers and civilians held as prisoners of war
or executed. An estimated 14,000 civilians charged with being disloyal were imprisoned in the
North, usually without a trial. Furthermore, thousands of avowed Unionists in the South had
all of their property seized by sequestration, and became homeless refugees.

Tens of thousands of Rebel civilians living in Northern states were made to leave
their homes, sometimes but not always having been given the choice of going North or
going South. In Missouri, Sherman's brother-in-law became enraged by rumors that residents
in the southwestern corner of the state were giving aid and comfort to guerrillas led by
William C. Quantrill. General Order No. 11, issued in March, 1863, by Thomas Ewing, Jr.,
depopulated four counties in a period of just 15 days.

Atlanta fell to men in blue when their commander was absent in the field. As soon as
he reached the Confederate rail center, he announced that he was turning it into a
permanent military base. Residents who had been ordered out of the city left by the train
load – but Sherman never took the first step toward turning the city into a Federal military base.

Tens of thousands of prisoners of war suffered indignities at the hands of their
captors, but the majority of them are known only by name and rank and regiment.
The remains of men who died in battle were often left to rot where they fell, and bodies of
hundreds of dead prisoners of war were stripped of their clothing and thrown into shallow
trenches without markers.

*Prisoners of war were frequently herded together in the open air, where they might spend days or
weeks before being shipped to a prison. These Rebels who were captured in Virginia's
Shenandoah Valley were photographed – under guard, of course – in May, 1862.*

LEFT: *Any time a region was occupied by the enemy, residents were likely to be given a few hours in which to get out. Dozens of southern villages, towns, and cities were depopulated by Federal commanders. Farmers and other rural folk often suffered the same fate; they loaded what they could on a wagon, turned their backs on their homes, and became refugees.*

BELOW: *Black refugees, most of whom were ex-slaves, were treated by Federal forces as contraband of war. After long hesitation in Washington, many males were accepted for military service. Females and children received little help of any sort; these contrabands were extremely fortunate to be given the use of an abandoned building. Many of these refugees found life in freedom to be more difficult than life in slavery.*

LEFT: *Some of the Confederates who were captured at Chattanooga, Tennessee, await shipment to the North by rail. Abraham Lincoln initially opposed any form of prisoner exchange, on the grounds that this would be tantamount to treating the Confederacy as a sovereign nation. Numerous cartels concerning prisoner exchange were later accepted by both sides, but the process was slow and cumbersome at best. Few photographs by Brady and his operatives exist of men after they became inmates of a prison; it is presumed that permission to take such photographs was seldom granted.*

RIGHT: *Rose O'Neal Greenhow, who posed for the photographer with her only daughter, came under surveillance by detective Alan Pinkerton before the Battle of Bull Run. When she was arrested and carted off to Old Capitol Prison, a search of her residence turned up stacks of correspondence with Washington notables. Her prominence put the Lincoln administration in a dilemma; an ordinary trial was out of the question because she might damage the reputation of highly placed officials. The president resorted to banishment as her punishment and ordered her to leave Union soil and remain off it for the duration of the war. In the South, she became a celebrity, a smuggler, and a blockade runner.*

LEFT: *Some prisons were open-air stockades that gave inmates no shelter or medical care and barely enough food to keep them alive. This rare photograph shows rations being issued to prisoners at Andersonville, Georgia, the most notorious of many bad prisons in the South.*

RIGHT: *Once the Capitol of the United States, this nondescript building became Old Capitol Prison soon after the start of hostilities. Many inmates of the prison had been charged – but not convicted – of harboring secessionist sentiments. An occasional celebrity was confined here for a time. Among these, the most notable was Washington hostess Rose O'Neal Greenhow, who is known to have transmitted important information to P. T. G. Beauregard and other prominent Confederates.*

LEFT: *Far the most notable prisoner photographed by a member of the Brady Studio was Jefferson Davis, ex-president of the Confederacy. Captured near Washington, Georgia, while trying to flee from the country, Davis did not go on trial. Instead, he suffered lengthy imprisonment at Fort Monroe, Virginia, where he was in close confinement for much of the time. He was eventually freed on $100,000 bail, secured for him by Horace Greeley and other prominent northerners.*

RIGHT: *While still a member of the Brady Studio, Alexander Gardner produced a stunning series of photographs that showed some of the many dead at Antietam. When this went on display in Brady's Broadway gallery, it produced a sensation. Until long afterward, it was not known that Gardner did not take his camera to men where they lay, but had them moved into positions calculated to produce dramatic photographs.*

RIGHT: *This group of officers sat on the court-martial of an unidentified prisoner who was a member of the Army of the Cumberland. Officers who went on trial rarely got a punishment more severe than dismissal from the military, but many an enlisted men was ordered to be "shot to death by musketry." Those convicted of desertion went to their deaths after an hour or two of hearings by a "drum-head court martial" hastily formed from a few officers who happened to be available. Brady may have pleaded with officials for an opportunity to photograph a firing squad in action, but probably was never given permission to record an activity about which military officials kept sparse records.*

LEFT: *This stark but stunning photo of unidentified Confederates was taken so that the tiny Dunker Church would loom in the center background of the Antietam battlefield. The nearly straight alignment of bodies suggests – but does not prove – that Alexander Gardner had these men dragged into position before his shutter clicked.*

RIGHT: *A dead soldier on the Petersburg battlefield. Numerous Civil War accounts include descriptions of what was then called "instant rigor mortis." According to reputable eyewitnesses, some men looked in death precisely as they looked an instant before taking a fatal ball or fragment of a shell.*

LEFT: *Close up, a single dead Confederate yielded a grimly dramatic photo. Placement of the two hand weapons hints that they were carefully arranged for photographic effect.*

LEFT: *Embalmers usually appeared a few hours after a major battle. Many of them used arsenic, which has remarkable preservative qualities. They demanded cash on the barrel head for their work, which meant they did not deal with bodies that had not been identified by friends or relatives. Many an embalmer had a sliding scale of charges, under which his fee rose rapidly if he was dealing with the body of an officer of fairly high rank.*

RIGHT: *Opposing forces withdrew from some battlefields so hastily that little or no attempt was made to recover and bury bodies of the fallen. These skeletons of some of the many men in blue who died at Cold Harbor in one of the most brutal charges of the war were retrieved after many months. Though many skeletons were retrieved for decent interment, the identity of these long-dead soldiers could not be known.*

RIGHT: *A grim view of a Union cemetery at City Point, Virginia, where some of the soldiers who had fallen in battle or who succumbed to sickness were laid to rest. Only some of the dead could be identified, their details crudely marked on simple "headstones."*

A LAND LAID WASTE

"Invaders are upon our sacred soil.
They plan to strip the countryside bare and to leave our cities in ruins."
C.S. General Joseph E. Johnston

Combat was directly responsible for surprisingly little destruction of property. Fighting men set out, however, to cripple the enemy by destroying bridges, railroads, and other components of the infrastructure. Much such devastation by Rebels took place when cities were abandoned. Spectacular photographs of fallen Atlanta include what was left of a long Confederate ammunition train. The train was destroyed by C.S. General John B. Hood in order to prevent the enemy from seizing carload after carload of ammunition.

Two examples of attempts by northerners to subdue the South by laying it waste took place very early. Knowing that secessionists of Virginia were approaching the vital Harpers Ferry arsenal, members of its garrison tried to burn the place to the ground. Soon afterward at the huge Gosport Naval Yard, also in Virginia, the commandant destroyed vessels, guns, and on-shore facilities before withdrawing. He botched his job, for spikes were easily removed from cannon and the partly burned U.S.S. *Merrimack* was used as the shell for construction of the ironclad C.S.S. *Virginia*.

Some of the work aimed at creating a scorched-earth wasteland was planned carefully and executed deliberately. Sheridan and his men moved into the Shenandoah Valley with the avowed goal of stripping it so bare that a crow couldn't survive in it. Sherman announced his plan to "make Georgia howl" before setting out on his March to the Sea.

Some wanton destruction without military purpose took place in retaliation for things done by the enemy. That was the case with Chambersburg, Pennsylvania. The once-prosperous town was deliberately leveled in order to "teach a lesson to Yankees who destroyed the Virginia Military Institute."

Collectively, the many works of destruction for a variety of reasons literally made a wasteland of much of the Cotton Belt in which secession was spawned.

Richmond's Galligo Mills is believed to have been a major producer of cloth used for making Confederate uniforms. Though Rebels who garrisoned the city knew that the war had been lost, in early 1865 they did their best to make these mills useless to the Federal forces who were only a few miles away from the Confederate capital.

LEFT: *Righting and repairing a derailed locomotive cost much more time and labor than restoration of a few miles of demolished track. During an attack on U.S. General John Pope's supply line, Rebel raiders managed to throw an engine on its side near Cutlet's Station, Virginia. An experienced crew probably spent almost a week getting it back in running condition. Shortly before or after this incident, executives of the U.S. Military Railroad decided to organize special units whose members did nothing but deal with wrecks.*

LEFT: *Demolition crews on both sides very quickly learned that it was easy to rip up rails in order to render a railroad inoperative. Soon it was learned that repairs could be made almost as rapidly – provided that rails remained undamaged. Because Sherman habitually destroyed rails by heating and bending them, a rail twisted beyond repair came to be called a "Sherman's necktie." Here, logs and iron have been put in place so that fire will make the rails pliable at their centers so that they could be twisted into useless scrap metal.*

LEFT: *Confederate cavalry effectively put an end to use of Mayo's Stone railroad bridge over the James River, not far from Richmond, in 1865. Repairs took longer than usual because the bridge had been so solidly built.*

RIGHT: *Quiet serenity belies the furious combat that had taken place earlier at this bridge inside White Oak Swamp in late June, 1862. A figure seated on the nearside bank surveys the scene of destruction as another standing on the other side makes a closer inspection. General George B. McClellan's Army of the Potomac had filed across the bridge, then demolished the structure in a bid to delay Stonewall Jackson and his men in gray. Jackson's men managed to get across the creek despite the fact that the bridge was useless, and a significant battle for possession of the crossing followed.*

LEFT: *Shells fired from both sides leveled a civilian's residence during the first significant battle of the war. Members of the Henry family occupied a spacious house that came under fire from both Federal and Confederate forces early on July 21, 1861. Mrs. Henry, matriarch of the family was carried to what was considered to be a place of safety but was brought back to her home before the battle ended. She was fatally injured by a fragment of a shell, and the Henry house was destroyed.*

RIGHT: *The sprawling Harpers Ferry arsenal, biggest installation of its kind south of Massachusetts, experienced little damage when its Federal garrison hastily left for Carlisle Barracks, Pennsylvania. During subsequent struggles for the vital area that included the arsenal, it was left with only portions of its walls standing.*

RIGHT: *Situated in a deep valley at the confluence of two major rivers, the town of Harpers Ferry was so located that Confederate and Union leaders staged a number of attacks against it. It changed hands several times, and during the struggles that revolved about it the once-splendid railroad bridge that was prized by residents of the surrounding region was rendered useless.*

RIGHT: *Charleston, South Carolina, fifth largest of Colonial cities, suffered light damage by comparison with the massive fort that once dominated its huge harbor. Federal forces took care, however, to render significant structures such as the depot of the North Eastern Railroad useless to Rebels.*

BELOW: *When opposing forces left the Bull Run battlefield, residents of the region found that they had to go miles out of their way in order to cross the stream that named the contest. Brady Studio operatives George N. Barnard and James F. Gibson are credited with having made this photograph.*

LEFT: *Commanders on both sides regularly took possession of the homes of civilians and used them as headquarters. U.S. General Ambrose Burnside seized the spacious Phillips house near Fredericksburg and used it during his disastrous assault upon the town. By the time the fighting ended, members of the Phillips family were refugees, dependent upon relatives for housing.*

LEFT: *Dejected Richmond residents can only stand and stare among the rubble that was Carey Street. There is little left of what was once a flourishing center of southern industry.*

RIGHT: *Charleston, South Carolina, residents embarked upon a program of restoration soon after peace was declared. Their severely damaged Circular Church, still standing, was the focus of an early program aimed at restoring it to its prewar glory.*

LEFT: *Though "the city where secession began" was far from destroyed, residential areas of Charleston suffered extensive damage from the Union's big naval guns plus special batteries that were erected on James Island. The specific role of the latter was to "throw sufficient shells into the city to make life in it unbearable." On at least two occasions in 1864, frightened residents fled from the besieged city in droves.*

RIGHT: *Most of the extensive damage suffered by the capital of the Confederacy was done by men in gray who were in the process of giving up the city and fleeing. The Virginia State Arsenal, photographed with the James River in the background, was too important to be left standing. This photograph has survived despite two cracks and a chipped spot in the collodion-coated glass plate.*

RIGHT: *Charleston's famous Mills House hotel (upper left in photo), which is still in use, may have been the target of Federal gunners who didn't know its exact location. Artillery leveled two or three adjacent city blocks. Selmar Rush Seibert, who is credited by the War Department Library with having made this photo in 1865, may have been one of many operatives who were paid and supplied with equipment by Brady.*

LEFT: *Union soldiers inspect what was left of the Virginia State Arsenal after a Confederate demolition crew had finished their work. Despite the massive destruction, at least two huge stacks of cannon balls remain in position, little disturbed.*

LEFT: *Early analysts of the massive collection of glass plates that were produced by members of the Brady Studio considered these Richmond ruins to have been the product of fire from heavy guns. Since Federal forces never shelled the Confederate capital, this is probably another example of damage that resulted from Rebels who did not want anything of military value to fall into the hands of the enemy.*

BELOW: *With enemy forces rapidly approaching Richmond and the Army of Northern Virginia having surrendered, Confederate authorities tried to ensure that all industrial buildings in the city were leveled. A huge water wheel seems to have escaped their destructive intentions, but the unidentified structure to which it was attached has been damaged beyond repair.*

RIGHT: *Columbia, the capital of South Carolina, suffered extensive damage during and immediately after it was occupied by Sherman and his Union troops. Analysts differ widely in their views as to whether Columbia was deliberately laid low by Federals or suffered severely from fires set by Rebels.*

LEFT: *A Federal sentry and a companion pose for the camera, sitting among the rubble of what is left of Richmond industrial buildings. What the trooper is guarding, or why, and against whom, are not known.*

RIGHT: *Behind the makeshift flagstaff can be seen the effects of Fort Moultrie's fire on the officers' quarters and sally-port of Charleston's Fort Sumter. Since the fort had not been designed to fire at "home territory," its guns and embrasures almost all faced out to sea.*

BELOW: *Little is known with certainty about Haxall's Mills in Richmond. This plant must have produced war materiel or other essentials, however. Confederates did their best to render it useless to Federal forces that were about to seize and occupy the city.*

PHOTOGRAPHING THE WAR

"...Brady has brought home to us the terrible reality and earnestness of war."
New York Times, reporting on Brady's
"The Dead of Antietam" exhibition, 1862

Brady and his operatives had to cope with numerous difficulties that never diminished. Time was at the top of this list. The photographer had to estimate how long to expose a negative. If it didn't get enough time, underexposure was inevitable; if he let the shutter remain open too long, overexposure resulted in a less than satisfactory negative. Time was a major factor with his subjects, as well. It was extremely difficult to persuade more than about half a dozen persons to "freeze" for two to four seconds. Animals rarely remain still for that length of time, hence they appear in only a few photographs taken during the war.

It took skill to smear a glass plate with a coating of collodion emulsion that was neither too thick nor too thin. After having been exposed, the wet plate had to be processed promptly in a mobile dark room. Once this was done, the fragile glass had to be stored so it would not break. Surprisingly few extant images made by members of the Brady Studio are cracked – and such damage could have been incurred weeks or months after the photograph was made.

Lacking anything remotely resembling a modern light meter, the photographer relied on his best judgment concerning intensity of light and prevalence of shadows. A trace of lint on an unexposed plate with a viscous coating could play havoc with results even if an exposure was precisely timed and lighting was ideal. Focal length had to be set properly by hand, or the photograph would be blurred. Facing an array of problems that do not exist for today's photographer, the real marvel of the work done by the Brady Studio is that so many thousands of images were preserved in reasonably good condition.

This is believed to be the first actual photograph of the U.S. Army in combat. It was made under fire by Mathew Brady at the Battle of Fredericksburg, Virginia, in 1863. Toward the end of the four-second exposure time, the cannon roared, causing Brady's camera stand to shake, such that blurring of the image occurred, especially of the mounted officer on the right.

LEFT: *Alexander Gardner, one of Brady's most talented operatives, photographed the president and General George B. McClellan conferring at Antietam about two weeks after the bloodiest day in American history. Experienced as he was, Gardner didn't get the light and exposure time right when he made this shot. At least one other photo made immediately before or after this one "came out just right."*

RIGHT: *This photo of U.S. Grant and a dozen of his officers plus an unidentified body servant who crept into the right background just before the shutter clicked is especially important. It shows Colonel Ely S. Parker, who was rarely photographed and was not identified by the camera man, just to the right of the tree in the middle. A full-blooded Seneca who was reared in New York, Parker was an attorney and engineer who met Grant in Galena, Illinois. Having been rejected for military service because of his racial background, Parker was brought into uniform by Grant and later became his military secretary. Parker wrote out the terms of Grant's surrender demand for the ceremony at Appomattox Court House. Robert E. Lee was reputedly taken aback by the presence of an officer he initially thought to be black. In later life, Parker's most prized possession was a carbon copy of the document he prepared for use at Appomattox.*

RIGHT: *Near Brandy Station, Virginia, Brady or one of his operatives caught sight of an unusually colorful group of men who belonged to a horse artillery brigade. The photographer may have carefully arranged for a black soldier to stand at the left as the photo is viewed and for a black contraband or body servant to stand at the extreme right. Excessive light bounced off the canvas tent at the right rear, but a fellow standing just to the left of the tent didn't get enough light.*

LEFT: *General John A. Dix, seated third from left in the photo, assembled 16 civilian members of the U.S. Sanitary Commission for a group photograph. Despite the fact that they were prominent business and professional men who listened carefully to instructions, the fellow at the extreme right simply couldn't "freeze" as instructed. Another shot of this group taken at the same time is even more badly blurred.*

RIGHT: *Tales according to which Mathew Brady's failing eyesight and other factors prevented him from personally making any of the Civil War photographs credited to his studio are patently erroneous. He positioned this group of officers carefully, set his camera, then casually leaned against the tree at the right in the photo in order to trip the shutter with the remote he held in his right hand.*

LEFT: *General U. S. Grant and eight members of his staff were captured on a plate that seems to have been given its coat of collodion too hastily or to have captured a few particles of dust while being put into place. Colonel Ely S. Parker, seated next to General John A. Rawlins, at the extreme right in the photo, was well below the defective or damaged segment of the glass plate.*

LEFT: *During the brutal 1862 battle of Fredericksburg, a group of men under the command of General Robert E. Lee assembled in an undamaged sector of the town during a burial cease-fire. Far away, across the Rappahannock River, Mathew Brady is believed to have climbed to the top of what was left of a railroad bridge. From this elevated perch, he made one of the earliest known photos obtained by means of a telescopic lens. It is also the only photograph in the field of Confederate forces made from the Union lines by a Union photographer.*

BELOW: *Limited ability to vary the focus of the camera hampered work done by a member of the Brady Studio on November 19, 1863. Members of a regiment are obviously marching down a street in the village of Gettysburg, on the way to the site where Lincoln delivered the Gettysburg Address. Though substantially more than 100 persons were before the camera, not a single face can be seen clearly.*

LEFT: *Some time after having surrendered at Appomattox Court House, Robert E. Lee accepted the presidency of what was then Washington University. Brady himself probably hurried to Richmond to get a photograph of Lee, the civilian, who agreed to pose wearing a military uniform. Unable to find a spot in the house where he considered the lighting to be satisfactory, the photographer persuaded the general/educator to stand before a door under the back porch of the Lee home.*

RIGHT: *A Mathew Brady photograph of two of his assistants resting for a "brew" at Petersburg, Virginia. A black aide settles the horses, which were notoriously difficult to photograph while still. Brady and his teams of operatives lived rough in the field, sometimes in danger of being caught up in the fighting. They carried all their photographic and processing equipment in carts, and also had the problem of preserving their exposed glass plates.*

RIGHT: *Regarded as of minor significance for decades, any Civil War photo made by a member of the Brady Studio is today valued. Regardless of its subject, it provides unique insight into the conflict in which more Americans died than during all other wars combined. This photograph was made quite early, since half a dozen members of Company I – probably a unit of the 12th New York – wear havelocks (cloth cap and neck coverings) made for them by patriotic women. These white kepis with long tails were touted as sure-fire preventives of sunstroke. Wearers soon found that they cut off circulation of air around the head and face, so dumped them. Paper was used to make a positive print from a Brady negative; badly torn, the paper positive was carefully restored and re-photographed to yield this view. It is probable that after having carefully arranged this large group of men, Brady or one of his operatives directed men to perch on roofs at each side.*

INDEX